DATE			
MAR 8 021			

BEYOND TIME MANAGEMENT
Organizing the Organization

JANE ELIZABETH ALLEN

Addison-Wesley Publishing Company, Inc.

Reading, Massachusetts • Menlo Park, California • New York
Don Mills, Ontario • Wokingham, England • Amsterdam • Bonn
Sydney • Singapore • Tokyo • Madrid • San Juan

Library of Congress Cataloging-in-Publication Data

Allen, Jane Elizabeth.
  Beyond time management.

  1. Organizational Effectiveness. 2. Time management.
I. Title.
HD58.9.A45   1986   658.4'093   86–1182
ISBN 0–201–15793–4

Cover design by Steve Snider
Text design by Chris Reynolds
Set in 11-point Trump Medieval by Neil W. Kelley

CDEFGHIJKL-MU-89

Third Printing, May 1989

To the memory of my mother Jane
and my great-grandmother Jane,
two women of extraordinary purpose and direction.

CONTENTS

INTRODUCTION 1

CHAPTER 1

The Power of the Telic:
Your Basic Drive to Organize 9

The Components of Organizing 10
There Is Organizing and There Is
Organizing 16
The Effect of the Telic in Your Work
Group 24
The Adaptive Nature of Work Groups 26
"Meaning"—After, as Well as before, the
Fact 28
The Main Point 31

CHAPTER 2

Theoretical Priorities,
or "What Do I Really Want?" 33

Goals Are Theoretical Priorities 35
Making Theoreticals Explicit for the
Individual 36
Making Theoreticals Explicit for the
Work Group 43
The Main Point 51

CHAPTER 3

Operational Priorities, or "What Am I Really Doing?"   53

The Nature of Priorities: A Recap   56

Making Operationals Explicit for the Individual   60

Making Operationals Explicit for the Work Group   62

Operational Priorities as Problem-Definers   63

The Main Point   64

CHAPTER 4

The Problem of Priority Dissonance   65

Why Does It Happen?   66

The Story of the Gym, the Popcorn, and the Paperback Thrillers   67

Getting Rid of Priority Dissonance   72

Priority Dissonance and Procrastination   77

The Main Point   79

CHAPTER 5

Organizing for Competing Goals, or "Keeping Peace in the Pantheon"   81

Goals as "Gods and Goddesses"   83

The Problem with "Getting It All Together"   85

Stirring Up the Furies   88

CONTENTS

So What Is to Be Done?   90
The Art of "Polytheistic Organizing"   93
Implications for the Work Group   98
The Main Point   100

CHAPTER 6

The Meaning of Meetings   101

The "Why" Of Meetings   103
Wedding the Values of Action and Relating   108
Some Marriage Counseling for Meetings   110
The Main Point   112
Where We've Been and Where We're Going   113

CHAPTER 7

Visual Stressors:
Out of Sight, Out of Mind   115

Mental Rehearsal   117
Eliminating Visual Stressors   119
The Main Point   122

CHAPTER 8

The Problem with "To-Do" Lists   123

Our Lady of Perpetual Lists   125
To-Do Lists Don't Prioritize, They
    "Criticalize"   126
To-Do Lists as Visual Stressors   128

CONTENTS

Without a To-Do List, What Am I to
   Do?   128
The Main Point   129

CHAPTER 9

Planners: What They Are and
    How to Use Them   131
What Is "The Book?"   133
What Every Good Planner Should Have   135
The Main Point   142

CHAPTER 10

Organizing the Organization:
    Some Closing Reflections   143
Sometimes It's neither the Individual nor
  the Work Group . . .   147
Corporate Culture Confusion: Priority
  Dissonance on a Grand Scale   151
In Closing . . .   153

APPENDIX A

Ten Adages to Organize By   155

APPENDIX B

Where to Get Planners   159

Introduction

A lot of managers have read a lot of books on time management. You may have read quite a few yourself. Time management has offered an arsenal of tips and techniques for setting priorities, handling interruptions, and running effective meetings. We have been told how to keep "to-do lists," fight procrastination, and eliminate paper pileups.

However, having read all these books, you may still have found yourself a player in a drama I call:

THE TIME MANAGER: A TRAGEDY

Once upon a time, there was a manager who was a firm believer in time management. Armed with techniques and tips, he valiantly entered his workplace, ready to "get organized." But he immediately hit a snag. His colleagues in the organization, the people he worked with and whose help he needed to get anything done, hadn't read any time-management books.

Undaunted, the manager bought copies of these books to give to his unenlightened fellow workers. He distributed these books fervently to his secretary, his comanagers, his boss. But his secretary didn't have the time to read it, his co-project manager lost it, and his boss didn't agree with it ("That kind of stuff's all right, but around here, well, we like to stay loose and informal").

The data processing manager offered a small ray of hope. She read it, agreed with it, and began to "prioritize."

Now, the time manager thought, now maybe we're getting somewhere. Together, the data processing manager and I will form a shining example of the benefits of time management. Together, we two will "get things done," the "right" things, and on time! He arranged to meet with the data processing manager to coordinate priorities.

Hope dimmed, however, when the two managers compared their to-do lists. His "C" priorities were her "A" priorities. Her "B" priorities were his "A" priorities. They negotiated a few changes. But basically, they couldn't agree on what was important.

After a few arguments over what should be done when (arguments that sounded uncomfortably similar to the spats they had *before* they started to prioritize), the data processing manager gave up her "A, B, C" system. She went back to "putting out fires" and doing what she could when she could.

But the time manager clung to his commitment to "being organized." He stuck with the principles of time-management training in the face of late reports from technicians, interruptions from other managers, and constant "go-nowhere" meetings with the boss. But it got harder and harder to keep his time-management system going. He was organized, but his organization wasn't. He went back to his trusty time-management books, looking for help. He found none.

WHERE DID THINGS GO WRONG?

Time management has not been used as widely or effectively in organizations as many had hoped. Why not?

Reflecting on my experiences with and in organizations, two reasons come to mind. First, time management requires independence. Time management assumes that each person has complete freedom to plan, choose, and act.

But those of us who work in organizations know that we are not independent. On the contrary, we are highly interdependent. We rely on the janitor, the technician, the accountant, the clerk, and all our other coworkers. Together, we form a "system."

A system is any group of elements that is composed of interdependent parts. Labeled "departments," "sections," "work teams," these systems need an approach to "getting organized" that includes the reality of working in groups.

For example, my ability to get a particular report generated by next Tuesday is directly connected to the engineer's production schedule, my secretary's vacation schedule, and my boss's meeting schedule. Any attempt at planning the completion of that report by Tuesday without synchronizing my plans with the plans of the other members of my system would be total folly. Yet time management has offered little guidance on how to bring about such synchronization.

Second, time management focuses on the individual. Up to now, time management has ignored a very important characteristic of human systems. The outcome or product of a group will be greater than (or at least different from) the sum of the contributions of each individual.

For example, a collection of efficient individuals does not necessarily result in an effective group. Although each staff member prioritizes, these priorities may clash. Although everyone institutes techniques for dealing with interruptions, definitions of what constitutes an interruption may differ. Even if each individual member of a work group adopted the gospel according to time management, there would still be a need to link these individual missionaries together in a way that achieved salvation for the organization as a whole.

4

Traditional approaches to time management have not taught us how to make these linkages. Real organization goes beyond simply organizing the individual. Real organization is a total process of organizing not only the individual but also the system to which the individual belongs. And organizing skills are what this book is all about.

WHAT ARE "ORGANIZING SKILLS"?

Organizing skills are the techniques needed to organize—that is, bring together ongoing, interdependent actions into meaningful sequences. These sequences, in turn, produce meaningful outcomes—meaningful for the individuals and meaningful for the organization.

Organizing is a process. It is the process of linking values, assumptions, and behaviors together in a purposeful way. The result of successful organizing is "order."

Order for me as an individual involves the arrangement of my behaviors, my space, the paper, and other physical objects in my life in such a way that they make sense to me and support my values and goals. In the same way, order for an organization involves the arrangement of people, time, space, paper, and other physical objects in a way that makes sense to all the members of the group and fosters the goals of the organization.

The process of making order is really a process of making sense. It is especially important in the workplace because, when healthy adults perceive a work arrangement as sensible, they will usually get things done, and get them done well. When healthy adults experience a work arrangement as nonsense, they will usually botch things up.

But order cannot be imposed on a group of individuals from outside. The creation of an "orderly" group through the blanket adoption or imposition of to-do lists or time logs or any other time-management techniques does not necessarily result in "order." That is, the arrangements may not make sense or be inherently meaningful to the individuals involved.

Victor Frankl, a noted psychologist, has observed that nonsense can be created, but sense must be discovered. Work groups must be allowed to discover their own sensible arrangements and techniques. Organizing is this process of discovery.

By the way, order does not always look "orderly," especially to persons outside the group. Boxes of stuff stacked against the walls may not look very tidy, but as long as the arrangement serves the values and goals of the group, as long as the arrangement makes sense to them, then that's order.

SO SHOULD YOU SPEND TIME READING THIS BOOK?

This book is about organizing skills. Organizing skills pick up where time management leaves off.

Organizing skills focus on:

1. You as an individual whose personal effectiveness is directly related to the actions of others.

2. You as part of a "system," a work group whose organizational effectiveness is directly related to the linkages among members of the group.

So you should read this book if:

1. You have been trying to get or stay organized, but something (or someone) always seems to get in your way.

2. Your work group has been trying to get or stay organized, but the members always seem to get in each other's way.

This book is addressed to all who wish to improve the order in their work and thus enhance the meaningfulness and joy in their lives. Because the book (probably) will be read by one person at a time, it addresses the singular *you* throughout. However, the thoughts are offered to the plural *you*, as well— work groups composed of persons trying to get something done, together, and maybe have a little fun in the process. Ideally, these groups (departments, boards of trustees, club officers, families) will read the book simultaneously, working back and forth between personal concerns and group issues, between organizing the individual and organizing the linkages among the individuals.

A WARNING

After reading this book, you and your work team may conclude that (1) your current methods for organizing make sense and are working, and (2) the methods your group is using are diametrically opposed to some of the techniques suggested in this book. In that case, *forget the book* and continue to *do what works*!

Don't meddle yourself or your organization into a mess. Critically pick your way through the ideas offered here. Try something only if you believe it will enhance "order"—that is, only if you believe it will create arrangements that strengthen your ability to make sense to yourself and your colleagues—because arrangements that make sense are what organizing the organization is all about.

CHAPTER 1

The Power of the Telic: Your Basic Drive to Organize

One aspect of human nature that has been reaffirmed over and over again in philosophy, psychology, literature, religion, even in recent findings in biology is this: human beings, when they are emotionally healthy, are telic. (*Telic* is simply another word for "purposeful and sense-seeking.")

Human beings have a natural desire to make sense. As psychologist Frank Barron put it, "Health is the moment . . . of making sense to ourselves and others."

Each of us has a natural tendency toward purpose—that is, toward getting somewhere or something. People are "goal-seekers," "goal-maximizers," "goal-creators." Our every action is intended to get us something or someplace.

9

Unfortunately, we are not always completely aware of the "what" or the "where." That is, we are not always conscious of the goals we are heading toward. As Yogi Berra is reported to have said, "If you don't know where you're going, you will probably end up someplace else."

This lack of conscious awareness is often at the heart of a lot of problems for ourselves and our work groups. I shall discuss this concern more fully in chapter 4.

However, whether we "know" what we're doing or not, we telic beings act out of "purpose and direction." We are always going toward something. We always end up "someplace, somehow."

Which brings me to Organizing Adage 1:

**We all use our time
to get something.**

THE COMPONENTS OF ORGANIZING

Organizing is the making of arrangements that facilitate purpose and clarify direction. Since we have a natural desire for meaning and purpose, we are always organizing. We are always arranging people, paper, physical objects, our space, and our time in order to get something or get somewhere and to make sense to ourselves and others in the process. I can summarize all this by making a key point: We are always organizing, all the time.

Organizing is part of our telic nature. We are always "making arrangements."

As modern citizens of the postindustrial age, we achieve purpose and direction in our lives by arranging and rearranging five key components:

- People (ourself as well as others)
- "Paper" (anything that represents or transmits information)
- Physical objects
- Space
- Time (which is really priorities)

Organizing people relates to arrangements for developing and influencing yourself and others to accomplish desired goals. The classic time-management discussions concerning procrastination, delegation, interruptions, and effective meetings in fact stem from our ongoing involvement with organizing people.

Organizing paper relates to arrangements for storing and retrieving information. Each piece of paper that comes into your life—a paycheck, a dry-cleaning stub, a flyer announcing 20 percent off this week at the car wash—carries a bit of information.

Organizing paper for most of us involves two steps:

1. We decide what to keep.
2. We decide where to put it.

First, organizing paper involves choosing which pieces of paper—that is, bits of information—make sense to you and will help you to get to where you believe you want to go. In my case, my paychecks make sense to me on one level because they are printed in my native tongue (English) and issued in my native currency (dollars). They also make sense to me because (most of the time) I see a logical connection between the work I've done and the remuneration I'm offered.

Moreover, the information on my paychecks helps me get to where I want to go (or at least lets me know if I can afford to go there). So I always decide to keep the piece of paper that is my paycheck.

Second, organizing paper involves designating a system for keeping the information somewhere until I need it (storage) and a system for getting at the information when I need it (retrieval). File cabinets, bookshelves, windowsills, computers, kitchen counters, vertical files, the refrigerator door, three-ring binders, wallets, coffee tables, end tables, night tables, dining tables, and the floor are all storage and retrieval systems. They each represent an attempt to organize paper—that is, put information someplace and get it back again.

Organizing physical objects relates to arrangements for deciding what things I need in order to achieve my goals. It also involves seeing to it that these items are available and functioning when I need them.

To achieve my goals of providing prompt, pleasant, individualized service and on-call availability to my corporate clients, I need (among other things) client status files and a telephone. The files need to be legible, and the phone needs to work. Organizing space relates to arranging the physical objects in my life. Organizing space involves relating the function of one item to the function of another.

In my office, the arrangement of space must permit me to open the drawer containing the client status files all the way. Otherwise, any client who calls and whose company name ends in T–Z has to endure many minutes of irrelevant conversation as I fumble to reach back into the drawer to get the file. Moreover, since I am left-handed, the phone had better be to the right of my desk and the files on the left. Otherwise, I end up garroting myself with the phone cord as I pass the phone from hand to hand in an attempt to pull files and take notes while talking with the client. And it's hard for a choking consultant to sound professional.

Organizing time relates to arrangements concerning what I wish to do and when I wish to do it. Organizing time actually involves choosing and arranging my priorities. Remember that, given our telic nature, we all use time to get something. Time, therefore, really represents the operationalizing of priorities.

This point is central to the development of effective organizing skills. The relationship of time to

13

priorities is so important that chapter 3 is devoted to the topic.

People, paper, physical objects, space, and time are all interconnected, interacting in "the system" that is you and that is your work group. Arrangements made in one area affect all the others. Changes in the arrangements of one result in changes in the arrangements of all the others.

For example, let's consider the story of the secretary, the interruptions, and the filing cabinets:

Muriel was a dedicated and efficient secretary. But Muriel was getting fed up. She provided administrative support to five middle managers. This "cluster" had recently been moved to a redesigned workplace in which the secretary's desk sat at the opening of a semicircle around which the managers' offices were located. The area against the wall behind Muriel's desk contained the filing cabinets and copy machine.

Muriel was upset because the number of interruptions to her work had risen 1000 percent since moving to the new workplace. Why? Well, the managers and their staffs frequently used the area behind Muriel's desk as a shortcut to get from one end of the cluster to the other. Meeting each other in this space, they would usually stop and chat for a few moments. If someone was using the copying machine, as well, a full-blown discussion generally emerged. Sometimes these comments related to work. More often they involved Monday night football, mortgage rates, and Christmas cookie recipes.

Since she was sitting right there, the managers, out of a feeling of cluster togetherness, usually invited Muriel into these chats. With this new social gathering place right in the middle of *her* work area, there were times when Muriel could barely hear phone conversations or get to the files because of the number of people congregated in back of her.

Muriel had taken to doing the filing late in the afternoon so she could roll herself over to the files on her filing chair without having to run interference worthy of a San Diego Charger. One evening, she forgot to roll the filing chair back to where she normally stored it near her desk. Instead, the chair remained out in the unofficial "corridor," sitting in front of a file cabinet.

The next day, Muriel noticed that the foot traffic and noise level behind her had dropped dramatically. She couldn't think of why until she went to do the filing at the end of the day. The filing chair was still sitting in front of the cabinet.

Muriel realized that the chair had effectively blocked people from going back and forth. The rearrangement of the chair redefined the space and rearranged the people. The space was no longer a thoroughfare. It was a filing and duplicating area.

She left the chair in front of the cabinets a few more days to see what would happen. Relative peace and order returned to Muriel's work area, and nobody moved the chair. Upon receiving assurance from the health and safety officer that it was OK to leave the chair there ("After all, it's not officially a hallway"), she knew that she had solved her people problem, and she hadn't uttered a word about it to the people; all she had done was move a chair.

This story is an excellent example of Organizing Adage 2:

> People and objects, space and time
> are interconnected.
> If you want to change the arrangement of one and can't,
> change the arrangement of another.
> It will help.

THERE IS ORGANIZING AND THERE IS ORGANIZING

Everybody organizes. But some organizing systems are functional, and some organizing systems are dysfunctional.

Functional organizing systems result in "order," arrangements that make sense. For arrangements to make sense, they must be linked to our beliefs, values, and goals. That is, the arrangements must help us to get to where we believe we want to go.

Dysfunctional organizing results in "disorder," arrangements that don't make sense. That is, these arrangements get in the way of our ability to get to where we believe we want to go.

Organizing People

An arrangement of people (myself and others) is functional when it provides:

1. Clear reminders of my objectives, what I wish to achieve.

2. Specific motivators or rewards to continuously guide my behavior toward those objectives.

Therefore, dysfunctional people-organizing may arise from:

1. Being unclear on what I wish to achieve.

2. Having no reminders, or inadequate reminders, of what I wish to achieve.

3. Lack of a reward system to continuously motivate me toward what I wish to achieve.

4. Having a reward system but one that rewards me for behaviors that have nothing to do with, or are directly antithetical to, what I wish to achieve.

Procrastination is one manifestation of a dysfunctional organizing system. We procrastinate, for example, when we are unclear on what our values and objectives are either as an individual or as a member of a work group. I discuss procrastination more fully in chapter 4.

Organizing Paper

A system for organizing paper is functional when it provides:

1. Clear guidelines regarding what information is important to me based on my values and objectives.

2. An effective system for storing desired information when received and retrieving desired information when needed.

Therefore, dysfunctional paper-organizing arises from:

1. Lack of clear guidelines for what to keep and what to throw away or pass on to others.

2. Guidelines that result in selections not in keeping with my values and objectives. (I throw away information that has meaning to me and would further my purposes. I keep information that has little or no meaning to me and/or would not serve my purposes.)

3. Lack of a system for putting the information someplace where I know where it is and can retrieve it easily when I need it.

Paper pileups and "lost" papers are manifestations of a dysfunctional paper-organizing system. Unsorted stacks of paper represent the failure to have or apply a decision rule regarding what information directly relates to objectives.

"Lost" papers are a result of failed storage and retrieval systems. The inside pocket of a coat jacket is an example of a storage and retrieval system that is usually dysfunctional. You may store information there. But frequently, the only person who ever gets to retrieve the information is your dry cleaner (and usually, he or she isn't interested in it because it doesn't relate to his or her *own* purposes or direction!).

Organizing Objects

A system for organizing physical objects is functional when it provides:

1. Specific indications of the items needed to accomplish my objectives.

2. Steps for obtaining these items and keeping them in good condition.

Therefore, dysfunctional organizing of physical objects arises from having:

1. No clear indications of what items are needed to achieve objectives.

2. Erroneous indicators—indicators that recommend items that have no relation to objectives or actually impede the accomplishment of objectives.

3. No mechanisms for effectively obtaining items.

4. Faulty mechanisms for obtaining items—the items obtained have no relation to objectives

or actually impede the accomplishment of objectives.

5. No schedule for maintaining the items in good condition.

Not having the right "tool" at the right time, running out of supplies at critical output points, and frequent equipment failures are manifestations of dysfunctional systems for organizing physical objects. Those of us who have ever failed to buy a service contract on a piece of equipment that subsequently forced us to readjust our entire production schedule due to breakdowns, or who bought a word processor rather than a small business computer (or vice versa) that would have more effectively supported our purposes, or who have missed a plane because our untuned car broke down on the way to the airport need no further examples of what dysfunctional organizing looks like in this area.

Organizing Space

Finally, the criterion for the functional organizing of space is simple, although it is frequently overlooked: Space is functionally organized when the arrangement of people and items in it supports my and the group's goals and objectives. Space is dysfunctionally organized when the relationship of people to objects and objects to each other impedes the functioning of the people and the achievement of objectives.

The organizing of space is closely linked with the organizing of physical objects and people: what do you have, and where do you put it for use by whom, when?

I have observed that the dysfunctional organizing of space has been at the heart of many problems that at first look like people, paper, physical-object, or priority issues. For example, during assessment of the organizing systems of one of my corporate clients, a theme emerged regarding the need for more file cabinets, particularly cabinets to store eighty-column computer printouts.

The printouts seemed to be everywhere: on desks, floors, cabinet tops. The beautiful picture windows placed in each office by some human factors-sensitive architect to enhance human motivation by providing vistas of the sylvan glades beyond? Blocked out by stacks of printouts on the windowsills.

There did indeed seem to be a real problem here. However, as I walked through the building, talking with staff, I noticed several interesting things:

1. A computer-printout file room did exist. Three walls were banked with file cabinets.

2. The same room also served as a staff lounge. Part of the fourth wall was covered with a small refrigerator, on top of which was a coffee maker and a hot water heater. Next to

the refrigerator were soda and juice vending machines. Lunchroom tables and chairs were in the middle of the room.

3. The majority of the offices were equipped with desks that had a file drawer designed to hold computer printouts. These drawers all featured a sturdy lock.

I asked whether the cabinets in the file room cum staff lounge were full. I was told, yes, they were all jammed. Then, on my second day on site, I was invited to take a coffee break with several staff members.

When we got to the lounge, we found that the coffeepot was nearly empty (coffee, *good* coffee, was an integral part of the culture and functioning of this firm). My hosts said, "No problem, we'll make some more," and proceeded to do so.

From the top drawer of one file cabinet came a tin of coffee, a package of filters, a measuring cup, and some cinnamon. I noticed the drawer also contained an impressive variety of plain teas, herb teas, bouillons, and instant soups. Another drawer held the sugar, artificial sweetener, stirrers, cream substitute, and lots of napkins, paper plates, and plastic utensils. A third drawer contained cookies, crackers, and other snacks, all hygienically enclosed in plastic containers.

The real eye-opener for me, however, was the mugs. As my hosts so proudly reminded me, real coffee deserves real cups. Two file drawers were taken up with a beautiful assortment of coffee mugs, including extras for guests like me. This rounded out the coffee-break provisions.

As I enjoyed a very delicious cup of coffee and some wonderful Scotch shortbread cookies (my favorite!), I looked around the room. There were no wall shelves, neither were there any wall cabinets (although there was ample space for both). In other words, in a space designated as being both a file room and a lounge, the lounge arrangements were dysfunctional. Therefore, the file arrangements had suffered.

My next day on site, I observed another interesting phenomenon. Besides good coffee, the culture of this firm also supported physical fitness. The company picked up half the tab for membership fees in a health club a short distance down the block. A number of staff members went there during lunch hour, and having received an invitation to join them, I came prepared on this day with my gym bag.

Just before one o'clock, I stopped by the office of my host. As she explained to me that we were going to stop by the offices of a few more people who were going to join us, she reached over, unlocked the computer-file desk drawer, and removed . . . her gym bag. Stops at the other offices revealed that her colleagues kept their gym bags locked in desk drawers, too.

The recommendations I made are probably fairly obvious to you by now. Wall cabinets and shelves were installed in the lounge (at a fraction of the cost of purchasing computer-printout file cabinets). Brief unit meetings were held to explain how the gym bags were contributing to the "storage" problem and to ask for suggestions. Most people realized that they really didn't have to lock up their gym bags ("Who would *want* to steal my sweat socks?"). They could hang their bags in the same place they hung their coats.

A few employees took lockers at the health club, and some people kept their bags locked in their cars. But everyone welcomed "finding" the file space and being able to look out their windows again. In conjunction with a few adjustments to reduce the actual output of paper, the pileups disappeared and the work space became functional.

THE EFFECT OF THE TELIC IN YOUR WORK GROUP

Every member of your work group (including yourself) is pursuing his or her own purposes and direction. But they may not be the same purposes or even the same direction.

Therefore, we must avoid falling for what economist Lester Thurow refers to as "the myth of the Lone Ranger," the myth that has beguiled classic time-management books and training. We cannot assume that, just because each staff member is goal-directed and motivated, everything will turn out well for the organization. On the contrary, as Thurow points out, human systems thrive only when they develop "forms of social organization to get people *to work together* in more productive ways."

The challenge in organizing the work group, then, is to design forms of social organization that link individual purposes to each other and to the purposes of the group in such a way that the entire battery of purposes is sensible (if not agreeable) to each person.

An unknown poet wrote, "The pitcher cries for water to carry and a person for work that is real." We telic beings "cry" for reality, meaning, and sense in our work. We will rebel against any social organizations or behavioral requirements that don't make sense to us, no matter how "orderly" they may appear on the surface.

Healthy organizations make sense to themselves (staff) as well as to others (customers and the world at large). A healthy, organized organization is achieved when each member of the work group:

1. Knows the reasons for various organizing arrangements.

2. Finds the reasons and arrangements sensible.

3. Believes the arrangements support, or at least do not hinder, the achievement of his or her own individual purposes.

To effectively organize our work groups, we need to effectively link our various individual purposes through arrangements of paper, people, priorities, physical objects, and space that have meaning for each of us. But how? Faced straight on, making arrangements that are consistent with the purposes of each work-group member may seem like an impossible task. But two observations may suggest a way out:

1. Work groups, like all human systems, have a high degree of adaptability.

2. Meaning can stem from after-the-fact understanding, as well as from before-the-fact expectations.

THE ADAPTIVE NATURE OF WORK GROUPS

Work groups are adaptable. They must be in order to survive the constantly changing demands on them from without and within (corporate directives, change in market demand, serious illness of a work-group member).

Frequently, these demands are equivocal. That is, they can be seen as having more than one meaning. For example, to the marketing director, a decrease in product demand may mean the old ad campaign has gone stale. To the director of R&D, the same decrease may mean the old product has gone stale.

A goal of a new ad campaign may therefore make

the most sense to the marketing director. A goal of a development design for product diversification may make the most sense to the R&D director. They clearly don't share the same goals.

Yet for the company to survive, it must respond to the decrease in product demand, and respond quickly. To do this, a highly adaptive system does not waste time trying to hammer out common goals. Rather, effective adaptability involves convergence on *common means* that will permit the divergent goals to be satisfied.

For example, the marketing and R&D directors may agree to support each other in a drive to reprioritize the operating budgets for the remainder of the fiscal year. By backing each other in getting their budgets increased, they converge on means— that is, more money.

The precedence of common means over common goals has been termed the "concept of collective structure" by psychologist F. H. Allport. Based on research in group formation and function, the "concept of collective structure" makes the point that people converge first on issues of means rather than on issues of ends.

People do not have to agree on goals to act collectively. What they do need is to be aware of each other's goals so they can make effective "means" arrangements and "trade off" resources effectively.

Karl Weick, in his book *The Social Psychology of Organizing*, sums up the idea of means convergence versus goal convergence nicely:

People can pursue quite different ends for quite different reasons. Partners in a collective structure share space, time and energy, but they need not share visions, aspirations or intentions. That sharing comes much later, if it ever comes at all [page 91].

And so we return to the question: How can we devise systems of organizing that link the telic beings who are our co-workers into an effectively organized group?

Well, one answer may be to identify common means which support individual goals, and then devise organizing systems which provide common means. Such organizing systems, that is, arrangements of paper, people, physical objects, space, and time, will then make sense to all of us because they represent means to the ends of each of us. It is by this linkage through common means that work groups can adapt to changing environments and get things done.

"MEANING"—AFTER, AS WELL AS BEFORE, THE FACT

The telic nature of human beings compels them to go back and impute meaning to acts that may have seemed "meaningless" to them at the time of action.

As I mentioned earlier, we do not always "know" what we're doing. That is, we are not always consciously aware of what values and purposes we are pursuing.

This fact is particularly true of work groups. In order to survive—that is, "justify its existence"—a work group has to keep doing something, although the rhyme or reason of that something may escape it at the time. As Weick quips, "Chaotic action is preferable to orderly inaction." He goes on to observe:

> When a group . . . is confused, the emission of actions that can be viewed reflectively increases the chances that the group may discover what it is doing. Thus, when there is confusion and some member of a group asks, "What should I do?" and some other member says, "I don't know, just do something," that's probably a much better piece of advice than you might realize. It's better for the simple reason that it increases the likelihood that something will be generated which *can then be made meaningful* (italics added) [page 245].

Thus, meaning can be something we go back and place on existent organizing systems, as well as being a catalyst for the effective design of new organizing systems.

Retroactive meanings make up a good part of what we have come to call "corporate culture." They may be reflected in such statements as:

> "We set up our filing system this way because . . ."
>
> "We run our meetings this way because . . ."
>
> "We've always done it this way because . . ."

Gaining agreement on "retroactive meanings" is another way to link telic beings into effective work groups.

No one may know or remember how a particular system for organizing people or paper or priorities came into being. But the staff may be able to agree, in retrospect, on *why* such arrangements were necessary. This agreement establishes a linkage of meaning among the group and renders the organizing systems more understandable—that is, more sensible—to telic natures.

Agreeing on a reason why certain arrangements were made in the past does not mean that the group accepts or agrees on the usefulness of the arrangements in the present. But from a linkage of agreement on past sensibility, the group has a foundation to discover or create common sense for the present. Once the purposes are discovered, the group may decide to keep the organizing systems as they are, or the group may decide to change the systems. Either way, discussion will be possible because the arrangements will have been rendered sensible by retroactive attachment of meaning to them.

You can link the various individual meanings your staff has placed on organizing arrangements in the present by surfacing and making explicit a common culture (or agreement or value) concerning the purposes the systems once served in the past. You may, for example, post a "feedback" question on the bulletin board, such as: "A lot of us are complaining that we have too many meetings.

Thinking back, why did we start having so many meetings?" (Be sure to leave room on the bulletin board for responses, and be sure people know that they don't have to sign them.)

From the various comments, you can begin to forge some common agreement on why frequent meetings once made sense. This agreement may or may not be based entirely on fact. It doesn't matter. What does matter is that once your work group can create a purpose that frequent meetings served in the past, it will be easier for them to discover and discuss what purposes frequent meetings are serving in the present. They may then want to devise some other more acceptable ways for achieving these purposes.

THE MAIN POINT

This chapter has been a discussion of the relationship of our telic natures to our organizing effectiveness, both individually and as members of work groups. Such concepts as "telic," "collective structures," and "retroactive meaning" may seem a bit esoteric or hard to digest. The main point, however, is simply this:

When we are healthy, we human beings act out of meaning and purpose. We organize our lives to achieve goals and to feel meaningful.

The way I arrange my time, space, papers, and the people around me reflects specific values and purposes. Whatever I'm doing, I'm doing for a reason. Every lost file, well-run meeting, forgotten appointment, successful delegation, overdue report is part of my telic—that is, purposeful—organizing system.

To evaluate the functionality of your organizing systems, you need to ask two questions:

1. Are the purposes that are being achieved by this system the purposes I really want to achieve?

2. Is this system the most effective, least stressful way to achieve my purposes?

To answer these questions, you need two important pieces of information:

1. What do I really want?

2. What am I really doing?

The next two chapters offer suggestions on how you might go about getting some answers.

CHAPTER 2

Theoretical Priorities, or "What Do I Really Want?"

Webster's Dictionary has defined goals as "the end toward which effort or ambition is directed; aim, purpose." Goals are at the hub of all human organizing. We telic beings are always organizing our lives to achieve ends, and we always end up with something.

However, effective organizing involves not simply ending up with something. Effective organizing involves ending up with something that I want, something that has value and meaning for me. To end up with what I want, I need to know what I want.

Each of us makes statements about what we want out of life. I call such statements "theoretical priorities." Theoretical priorities are my values and preferences concerning what I want to achieve and how I want to achieve it. Comments such as "I definitely want to move to the top of this department," "I put my family first," and "Physical fitness is really important to me" are all examples of theoretical priorities. They are statements of what I believe I want at the time.

To organize effectively, however, it is essential to state these theoreticals explicitly, clearly, and completely—with special emphasis on completely. Otherwise, you will be expressing what you want in piecemeal fashion. And piecemeal prioritizing leads to piecemeal organizing.

For example, I may often state, "My family comes first." On the other hand, I may also frequently say, "I definitely want to move to the top of this department." Now obviously, I don't (can't) say both of these things at the same time. However, unless I set down a complete statement of my values for the various aspects of my life, I may not be aware that I am saying both of these things at different times.

It may be possible both to put my family first and to rise to the head of my department. However, if I don't "know about"—that is, if I am not aware of—my stated preferences for both, I may end up with organizing systems that support one "theoretical" at the expense of another. I then find myself saying one thing but doing something else. This can make me feel slightly crazy. I shall talk more about this predicament in chapter 4. However, I believe it's safe to say without elaboration that "slightly crazy" is not such a good way to feel.

So it's essential to state clearly what my theoretical priorities are for my job, for my family, for my body, for my mind, for each aspect of my life. When I know these theoreticals, then I know what has value for me. And when I know what has value for me, I have some sense of what to "do" in terms of organizing. Which brings me to Organizing Adage 3:

If you want to know how to organize your life, look at what's important to you.

GOALS ARE THEORETICAL PRIORITIES

Goals are statements of what's important to us. They define what we believe we wish to accomplish in our lives. Goals are what we are organizing—that is, making arrangements—for. (Goals are also the outcomes of our arranging, but I'll discuss that in the next chapter.)

Theoretical priorities are also statements of purposes or objectives I believe I want to achieve. That is, the product of goal setting is a set of theoretical priorities. Therefore, formal goal setting is one of the most effective ways to develop an explicit, clear, and complete statement of my theoretical priorities.

We have been told over and over again in various books and workshops that if we wish to get organized, we have to set goals. But rarely have we been told, or understood, why. Therefore, being the healthy, telic creatures that we are, we usually don't do it.

My discussion of our telic nature in the last chapter and theoretical priorities in this one is an attempt to clarify why goal setting is essential to effective organizing. Remember, you are always organizing your life toward the achievement of some ends. The ends you believe you wish to achieve are your "theoretical" priorities. To be an effective manager, you need a clear and complete statement of your theoretical priorities. The outcome of formal goal setting, properly done, is a set of clear and complete theoretical priorities. Therefore, goal setting is essential to effective organizing because it produces a set of statements (theoretical priorities) that make explicit your beliefs regarding what you are organizing for. Goal setting allows you to tell yourself (and others) what you really want in a coherent manner.

MAKING THEORETICALS EXPLICIT
FOR THE INDIVIDUAL

If you wish to surface and make explicit your own theoretical priorities, the best approach is to complete a formal goal-setting program. An enormous number of books and workshops are available that offer a wide array of techniques and exercises for setting goals. Therefore, I shall not go into a detailed "how-to" account here. What I shall do, however, is offer some general guidelines and a few exercises that may help you select a goal-setting book and/or workshop and get started.

First, be sure that any book or workshop you select provides you the opportunity not only to learn how to identify your goals but to actually identify some (if not all) of them. This is a subtle, but important, difference. Many of us have sat in workshops that showed us what to do. But when we got out of the workshop, we didn't do it.

So the best and most effective way to set goals is to set goals, not just learn how to set goals. In terms of workshops, this means that one-day programs will probably not be very effective. Even though they are more costly at the outset, multiple-day sessions of goal-setting training, ideally with opportunities for homework in between sessions, may be more cost-effective because you are more likely to get what you paid for: a clear, written set of goals.

Regarding books on goal setting, it is best to choose works that have a number of specific paper-and-pencil exercises for you to complete. Again, you can best learn how to identify values and set goals by actually identifying them and setting them.

Second, be sure that whatever goal-setting program you choose either starts or ends with values clarification. As I stated at the beginning of this chapter, goals are ends toward which we direct effort or ambition. Logically, the telic human being directs effort and ambition toward ends that are important to him or her. Certain ends are pursued as important because they enable the individual to maximize certain personally held values. Ervin Laszlo, in his description of human systems, observed this link between goals and values when he commented, "Nothing that pursues a goal is value free."

Values clarification is essential to goal setting, therefore, because when we know our values at any given point in time, we then have an indication of what goals or ends or purposes may satisfy us (or dissatisfy us) at that and future points in time.

Goal setting is always a projection. It is a projection of my present values onto my future outcomes. Of course, by the time the goals are achieved, my values may have changed. I may attempt to maintain certain organizing systems long after the goals they were intended to help me achieve have ceased to have any real value to me.

This type of dislocation frequently occurs at points of developmental crisis. For example, for the mature person, it may occur as the individual attempts to move from growth through fast-paced achievement to growth through increased self-acceptance. For an organization, it may occur as the organization attempts to move from growth through coordination to growth through collaboration.

In both cases, changing values can be a serious source of disorganization for both the individual and the work group. Thus, not only is it important to clarify values, but it is also important to clarify values regularly, particularly at points of developmental crisis, and be ready to adjust your goals accordingly. I shall discuss the relationship of organizational development to disorganization more fully in the last chapter.

I mentioned earlier that one can either begin the goal-setting process with values or end the goal-setting process with values, but in order to accurately identify one's theoretical priorities, values have to be clarified at some point. Let me now elaborate a bit on one approach to this process.

Some Goal-Setting Exercises

In my consulting work, I suggest to my clients that they think of goals as being of three types: life goals, five-year goals, and six-month goals.

- Life goals are values. They are statements of abstractions that are important to you.

- Five-year goals are objectives. They are statements of concrete outcomes you wish to accomplish.

- Six-month goals are behaviors. They are statements of observable, measurable actions you wish to perform.

In the goal-setting process, you may wish to start with life goals—that is, with values clarification. Based on these values, you can then generate five-year goals, a set of objectives or accomplishments that will support and reflect these values. Finally, based on your stated objectives, you can design your six-month goals, specific behaviors that will move you toward your objectives.

But some of you may have a hard time beginning the process with so awesome a concept as "life." For you, it's much more comfortable to talk about what you wish to do within the next six months. So you can start there. Set six-month goals every six months. After eighteen months, go back and review the goal statements you made and whether you achieved the goals or not. Look for patterns— what you've done, what you haven't done. Ask yourself the question, "If I were to continue this pattern of behavior for five years, what would I accomplish? What objectives would I meet?"

This review gives you a boost into five-year goal setting. From the objectives you choose, you can then extrapolate what values are important in your life, at least at this point in time.

Whether you start with "life" or with "six months," it's important to start. As I mentioned earlier, there are numerous books and workshops that will take you through a goal-setting program. However, to get you started, here are three goal-setting exercises:

The One-Hundred Years-Old Exercise

Imagine that you have been fortunate enough to live to be one hundred years old with a healthy mind and body. On your one-hundredth birthday, the local radio talk-show celebrity comes to your house to interview you. She asks you the question, "Looking back over your life, what five things are you the most proud of?" What would you like to be able to say? (Be sure that you make at least one response for each of the separate aspects of your life: family, personal, and professional. No fair making five statements about your children.)

What Do I Want My Life to Be Like in 199X?

Objectives can frequently be formulated by generating a large set of questions concerning what you want in your life five years from now and then answering the questions. Make your questions as specific as possible. Here are some examples:

Five years from now, what do I want my personal life to be like?

- What do I want in terms of friends in 199X?
- What do I want to look like in 199X?
- What skills and educational accomplishments do I want to have in 199X?
- Where do I want to be living in 199X?

Five years from now, what do I want my work life to be like?

- What do I want my job title to be in 199X?
- Where do I want to be working in 199X?

- What do I want my annual income to be in 199X?

- What associations do I want to belong to in 199X?

- What awards do I want to earn by 199X?

Five years from now, what do I want my family life to be like?

- If my parents are living, what responsibility do I want to take for them in 199X?

- If I am single, do I wish to be married by 199X?

- If I have no children, do I wish to have children by 199X?

- If I have children (especially teenagers), do I wish to have them all out of the house and then move to a one-bedroom condominium with no pull-out couch by 199X?

Writing the Four Key Elements

Six-month goal statements should be written to include four key elements:

1. Result desired
2. Minimum acceptable standard
3. Target date
4. Maximum cost in time and money

For example, a professional six-month goal might be:

> "I shall increase the average order my customers place [result] by at least 5 percent [standard] no later than April 30 [target date] at a cost not to exceed $250 and sixty hours of my time [cost]."

A personal six-month goal might be:

> "I shall meet three new people [result] with whom I'd be happy to spend at least a few hours each week [standard] before November 15 [target date] at a cost not to exceed $90 and fifteen hours of my time [cost]."

Remember, six-month goals are specific, observable behaviors: "meeting three new people," "increasing the average order placed by my customers." Try to identify at least one six-month goal for each of your five-year objectives.

MAKING THEORETICALS EXPLICIT
FOR THE WORK GROUP

The theoretical priorities of the individual may be formally stated as the goals of the individual. The theoretical priorities of the work group may be formally stated as the points of convergence among the individual "theoreticals" and with the stated goals of the organization.

To arrive at the theoretical priorities of the work group, therefore, we need three pieces of information:

1. The goals of the work-group members.

2. The goals of the organization

3. The points of convergence and divergence among these goals.

The Goals of the Work-Group Members

First, individual members need an opportunity to identify their own work-related values and goals and then, most important, share this information with each other in a safe and accepting environment. All too often, the group manager is the only member of the group who has any sense of the values and aspirations of each of the other members. And in this case, each staff member frequently has no clear idea what the manager's values and goals are for him or her.

The sharing of specific six-month behavior goals or longer-term objectives may not be wise, given the potential for competition and jealousy within groups. However, people usually are willing to talk freely about their values. Since values are at the root of all objectives and behaviors anyway, it is both feasible and effective to regard the theoretical priorities of work-group members as the occupational values each person holds at the time.

For instance, "Examining Your Occupational Goals," an instrument I designed for use in my consulting practice, is a simple yet powerful means for bringing occupational values to the surface. Individual members of the work group, including the manager, rank thirteen work-related values. Some of the values are:

- Challenging problems: a constant involvement with complex questions and demanding tasks.

- Job tranquillity: a lack of pressures in job role and work setting.

- Friendship: close relationships developed as a result of work activity.

- Individual achievement: total responsibility for projects.

Ranking the thirteen values takes about ten minutes. Then, in a group discussion facilitated by a nongroup member, individuals compare and contrast rankings. The discussion is usually very illuminating, both individually and collectively.

Take, for example, "The Case of the Lone Duplicating Machine":

The staff of the purchasing department was uncomfortable. For years, each person had done his or her own duplicating work and had done it on the only duplicating machine in the department, which was located in a small alcove at the end of the hall. Then Tom joined the staff. Almost immediately he began pointing out that the duplicating procedure seemed very inefficient (he had just finished reading a time-management book). Tom noted that he, and everyone else, spent a lot of time walking back and forth to the duplicating machine, as well as waiting to use the machine if someone else was there first.

True, when people had a rush job and the machine was in use, they simply took the job next door to the machine in payroll. And purchasing always seemed to be on schedule with its work. Yet Tom's observations did make his colleagues feel a little guilty. Maybe they were "disorganized."

Tom suggested that the department either lease another duplicating machine (and put it at the opposite end of the section from the first machine to cut down on walking) or assign one of the clerks the function of duplicating.

Nobody liked the second idea, but everybody acknowledged the logic of the first. They were the purchasing department. Finding the budget and making the arrangements for leasing a duplicating machine would be a snap for them. But two months went by, and nobody did anything about it.

It was around this time that the purchasing department participated in the organizing-skills training program that was being offered by their company. The department felt pretty together on the whole. But they understood that the training would help them identify and assess their organizing systems, reinforcing those systems that were working and suggesting guidelines for adjusting those that were not. Besides, in the back of their minds, nearly everybody was feeling uneasy concerning the matter of the duplicating machine.

As part of the training, the group completed the "Examining Your Occupational Goals" exercise. And a very interesting fact emerged: everyone had "friendship" (close relationships developed as a result of work activity) as one of their top four values.

When the facilitator reminded the group that one criterion of an effective organizing system is that it supports values and purposes that the group shares, Harold thought of the duplicating machine. "You know," he chuckled, "I think one reason I like the duplicating arrangement the way it is is because it gives me a way to informally stay in touch with everybody while still doing my work." Marcia agreed. "Also," she added, "some of my best ideas for working with vendors have cropped up while chatting with you all around the copier." "And I get to say 'Hi' to everybody at least once a day as I walk through the department to get to the machine," Ramon observed.

The group was silent for a few seconds. Several people glanced at Tom out of the corners of their eyes. "One of the reasons I transferred to this department," Tom said, "was because it seemed like such a friendly place to work. I admired purchasing's reputation for having fun and getting the job done well, both at the same time. We've been talking here about how an effective organizing system is one that supports the values of the group and enables it to do its work. Well, the duplicating setup may not be what some would call 'efficient,' but I think I can see how—for our group, at least—it certainly is effective."

The Goals of the Organization

The theoretical priorities or goals of the organization are presented in the organization's statements concerning what it believes in and where it wishes to go. These statements are found in such documents as the business plan, budget proposals, and strategic-planning documents. As a matter of fact, strategic plans may be regarded as formal statements of an organization's theoretical priorities.

It's important to remember at this point that an organization does not have to achieve, or even be working toward, a goal in order to have that goal. In other words, an organization can say it wants to move in any direction it wishes. Whether it is actually moving that way may be another matter. But with theoretical priorities, we are interested in where the organization believes it wants to go. We are interested in stated goals.

The issue of operational goals, what the organization really is doing, will be discussed in the next two chapters. For the moment, however, we are concerned with an organization's theoretical priorities, the goals the organization says it wishes to achieve. Effective organizing requires that the goals and values of the organization be known and understood by each of its members. There is then more likelihood that members will construct organizing systems that are compatible with the goals and values of the organization.

Yet it is amazing how few employees are briefed on their company's five-year plan, or on the budget proposals, or on the income projections, or on anything. Such formal discussions of theoretical priorities are usually reserved for upper management. The rest of the staff is left with gossip and scuttlebutt and, in turn, puts together organizing systems that reflect just that.

Sometimes whole departments are left out. Donald Petersen and Robert Malone have observed that, although chief executives repeatedly cite human relations as a major problem in their organizations, the human resources development department is frequently excluded from top-level discussions regarding corporate objectives and goals. Petersen and Malone rhetorically ask, "What percent of time does top management give to the chief personnel executive?"

Although you may not be a top executive, privy to your company's strategic plans, you do (hopefully) have some ideas concerning what is expected of your department for the next six or twelve months. To increase the organizing effectiveness of your work group, present these theoretical priorities to the group—the entire group: clerical, technical, administrative. Be sure you present not simply the goals, but the reasons behind the goals. (Remember the telic need to "make sense.")

If you don't know the reasons, or the reasons don't make sense to you, then go to *your* boss to straighten it out. If you can't get a clear explanation from your boss, and therefore can't give one to your staff, you can expect a wide discrepancy between the arrangements of people, paper, time, space, and physical objects the department needs to meet its goals and the arrangements the department actually ends up with. Since your staff won't know what they're making arrangements for, or why, they will probably make arrangements that achieve "something else."

Let me hasten to add that the staff may not always like the goals and explanations you present to them. For one thing, the departmental theoreticals may diverge drastically from the goals of some of the individual members.

However, these differences will at least be explicit and clarified rather than implicit and muddled. With these facts right up front, the group can then negotiate points around which a functional organizing system can be constructed.

If you feel you need help in developing the skills to carry out such negotiations, a number of training programs are available. For example, the Performance Management Workshop, offered by Finn Associates, Inc., teaches skills for coming to agreement on goals and priorities. As Libby Finn, president of the firm, has observed, "The single most important step in optimizing performance at work is having a clear understanding of how your goals relate to the goals of the organization."

The Points of Convergence and Divergence

Looking at your goals, the goals of your colleagues, and the goals of your organization, you may find many points of agreement. That's good. These points of convergence will represent your commonly held theoretical priorities.

However, upon reviewing those same goals, you may also find many points of disagreement. That is not so bad as it may at first seem.

I would simply ask that you think back to the last chapter. Remember that it is not necessary to get agreement on ends. All members of your work group do not have to share the same goals, neither with each other nor with the organization as a whole.

Effective organizing requires an awareness of divergent goals. Then these goals can be related through the construction and implementation of common means. Functional organizing systems are created around making arrangements of people, paper, space, and physical objects that, in fact, are common means to diverse goals.

THE MAIN POINT

Theoretical priorities reveal to us our goals, both as individuals and as an organization. By identifying where we want to go, we can then determine various ways to help each other get there.

Whether or not these "ways," or organizing systems, do, in fact, get us where we believe we want to go is, however, another question. Whereas theoretical priorities are statements of what I want

51

to do, operational priorities are statements of what
I am actually doing. To get a clear picture of the
effectiveness of my organizing systems, I need to
know both. And so I shall now turn to a discussion
of "operationals."

CHAPTER 3

Operational Priorities, or "What Am I Really Doing?"

The phrase *time management* turns off a lot of managers these days. Faced with problems of disorganization in their work groups and in their own personal lives, managers have found that, as solutions, the techniques offered by time management often just don't stick. In fact, people frequently avoid using them at all.

But it's difficult to apply solutions effectively when the problem isn't clearly understood. I believe that this is why time-management techniques have been so widely ignored or misapplied. Managers and employees have been offered solutions for disorganization, but they have been given little guidance on how to correctly identify and understand the problem of disorganization. (Re-

53

member the "tragedy of the time manager" in the introduction.)

This is a curious state of affairs. Over and over again, managers have been told: "Analyze and define the problem situation before you attempt to implement any solutions. A problem well defined is a problem half-solved."

Now effective problem definition requires that you first gather information about the troubling situation. Upon sensing that something is wrong, you set out to define with facts and figures exactly what that "something" is. You ask questions, review records, measure space, gather observational data.

The intent of this stage of problem solving is to determine:

- *Who* is involved in the troubling situation?

- *What* episodes or elements make up the troubling situation?

- *When* does the troubling situation occur?

- *Where* does it occur?

- *What* happens?

However, when managers become aware of a troublesome situation involving disorganization, do they then set out to ask the questions of who, what, when, and where? Well, usually not.

Generally, they take statements of the symptoms of the problem as definitions of the problem itself, without further investigation. Hearing (or uttering) a growing crescendo of complaints, such as "We can't seem to meet deadlines around here" or "I can never lay my hands on the daily production sheets when I need them" or "These meetings are going on and on and on!" the managers rush themselves (or their secretaries!) off to a time-management workshop to "get some answers."

Yet what the staff really needs at this stage is help in getting at the right questions, the questions of who, what, when, and where. These questions are aids in accurately formulating the problem. This formulation must come before those involved can validly choose and implement solutions.

Most time-management training does not offer the perspective of time-management techniques as tools in *problem finding*. Lacking this perspective, managers apply the techniques as solutions to poorly understood problems. The result: a large group of people who are discouraged, disgusted, angry, and bored with time management—people who have abandoned these so-called solutions as another waste of time.

The technique of time analysis is a good example of this crisis. Time analysis involves the recording of your activities over a period of time. This technique tells you "what you are really doing." Time analysis is usually conducted through time logs.

Managers have heard a lot about how the time-analysis approach can solve problems for them and their work groups. "Simply keep a time log. Look at it and you'll know what to do."

But time analysis doesn't solve problems. The information gathered from a time log is neutral information. For example, managers have been told that time logs reveal "time-wasters." But what is a "time-waster"? There is no absolute definition of *time-waster*. Merely looking at a time log will not, in and of itself, identify your time-wasters (or time-savers, for that matter).

Time analysis makes sense only when it is seen as a means of giving us information about our priorities. Our interest is not in time-wasters and time-savers. Our interest is in priority-minimizers and priority-maximizers. The information from a time log is therefore important not because it's a measure of time but because it's a measure of priorities.

That is, time analysis helps us to *find* important problems in the area of our priorities.

THE NATURE OF PRIORITIES: A RECAP

There are two types of priorities. The first type I call "theoretical priorities." The second type I call "operational priorities." Theoretical priorities were discussed in the last chapter. As you recall, theoretical priorities refer to the rank-ordering of my goals and values. If I set the goals of my department at a 150 percent increase in telephone sales within the next twelve months, then telephone talking is a high theoretical priority. If the objectives of my department call for automation and the phasing out of virtually all of the nontechnical employees, then nontechnical-employee development is a low theoretical priority.

The second type of priorities, operational priorities, are my activities ranked on the basis of how much time I spend on each one. If I spend 50 percent of my work hours on the telephone, telephone talking has a high operational priority. If I spend 2 percent of my work hours developing employees, employee development has a low operational priority.

Recall that:

• Goals are theoretical priorities.

• Time use is operational priorities.

and that, according to Organizing Adage 1:

We all use our time to get something.

Thus, operational priorities are the goals we are fulfilling with our behaviors. Operational priorities indicate what we are "getting" with our time.

Our behaviors are manifestations of important priorities because *that's what we are choosing to do with our time.* We each have priorities we are going after every minute of our lives. We are, at this level, not setting priorities. We are, instead, acting out priorities. Which brings me to Organizing Adage 4:

If it doesn't make sense to you,
you won't do it.
And if you're doing it,
then, at some level,
it *is* making sense to you.

Problems of disorganization arise when we become unaware of what we are doing, the purposes we are actually fulfilling. We may be placing high operational priority on objectives that, upon inspection, have no correlation to our theoretical priorities—that is, to our consciously stated goals and purposes.

For example, I may have a five-year objective of holding a position of national leadership in my professional organization. This objective supports the high priority I presently place on the values of recognition and achievement.

However, a time analysis of my activities over the past six months may reveal that I have used less than 1 percent of my time for professional organization activities. I missed the last regional meeting because of "conflicting appointments." (*Note*: The dates of the regional meeting had been announced to members over a year ago. Yet I chose to schedule a conflicting activity.) I declined invitations to review applications from prospective members because I was "too busy."

I can easily see that if I continue with this pattern of time use, there's no way my objective will be reached. The time analysis clearly shows that for the last six months, at least, I have not been using my time to gain leadership in my professional organization.

But how *have* I been using my time? Remember: "We all use our time to get something." The time analysis shows me what I'm not doing, true. But equally important, the time analysis shows me what I am doing.

A review of the time analysis for the same six months may disclose that I spend nearly 20 percent of my time giving talks to professional groups and writing. I observe that whenever I'm offered the opportunity to talk with a group or write an article, I take it. An article deadline, for example, was the main reason I was "too busy" to review prospective-member applications.

Looking at the whole matter objectively, I'd have to say that at some level (the operational level), giving talks and writing articles is pretty important to me. These activities are definitely more important to me, operationally, than gaining leadership in my professional organization.

So I am led to Organizing Adage 5:

> If you want to know what's important to you, look at how you use your time.

Writing and talking are important to me because that is how I am choosing to use my time right now. And the interesting thing is that, if I continue with this pattern of operational priorities, I may reach objectives (national talk-show star, author of a blockbusting best-seller) that will, in fact, support my values: recognition and achievement. However, until I am clear and conscious that the way I am actually going in fact may indeed be the way I really want to go, I cannot set up the most effective organizing systems for getting there. For example, I may have allotted several file drawers to professional organizational materials, drawers that are nearly empty. Meanwhile, I may have set aside only one drawer for writer's guidelines and correspondence with editors, and this drawer may be full and overflowing into a growing mound of papers on the floor.

MAKING OPERATIONALS EXPLICIT FOR THE INDIVIDUAL

Time-analysis techniques, such as time logs, tell us what our operational priorities are.

Many of us have balked at keeping time logs when it has been suggested in the past. The classic retort is, "I don't have time to keep a time log."

However, I believe that if we understand the sense of time logs—that time logs give us enlightening, motivating, and frequently gratifying information about what's important to us—then we will be more inclined to "make the time" to complete them.

If you do decide to keep a time log, use any format that feels comfortable to you, but be sure your analysis follows these guidelines:

1. Keep the log for at least three days, ideally seven days. Be sure the span of time you choose for keeping the log covers at least one nonwork day and one workday.

2. Keep the log from 7:00 A.M. to at least 9:00 P.M. Be sure you log in "personal" and "family," as well as "professional," activities.

3. Use time blocks no shorter than half an hour and no longer than three hours.

You may wish to do a three- to seven-day analysis each month for several months. Such an approach will give you real insight into the pattern of your operationals.

When you analyze the time log, you will probably find some surprises. One client was surprised to see how much time she spent "skimming" professional journals and other publications that came across her desk. Another client was shocked at the amount of time she devoted, in a given seven-day period, to caring for her physical appearance.

Please remember that "surprise" and "shock" do not imply that there is something wrong with these activities, that they are "time-wasters" of some sort. Rather, these reactions relate to the discovery of priorities the individuals didn't know they had. Whether the individuals choose to continue these priorities or not is another question. Sometimes the information from a time analysis is simply validating. We find we are spending time on those things we thought we were spending time on. However, that doesn't mean these activities are necessarily good. It all depends on whether or not they support our "theoreticals."

MAKING OPERATIONALS EXPLICIT FOR THE WORK GROUP

To find out how your work group is using its time, you can take one or both of two approaches:

1. You can summarize the data from individual time logs.

2. You can construct a work-group Time-Analysis Worksheet. This worksheet lists predefined task categories. Group members are asked to check the appropriate category at various points in the day.

Whichever approach you use, if you wish to obtain valid measure of operationals, you must be aware of and sensitive to a cardinal principle of work-group time analysis: Information about time use must not be employed as evaluation of time use.

If the members of your work group begin to suspect, in the slightest way, that time-analysis information will be used to rate them and/or their job performance, you will get inaccurate information or no information at all.

How can you increase the probability that work-group members will work with you in identifying the group's "operationals"—that is, what the group is really doing? Well, first of all, discuss with the group what "operationals" are all about. Explain how operationals are the other half ("theoreticals" being the first half) of the important information you all need to analyze and improve, if necessary, your organizing systems.

Second, whenever possible, collect the information anonymously. Since you are interested in aggregate, not individual, data, there is no need for names.

Sometimes, however, the nature of the activities will tell you whose log you are reading. Then you may wish to construct a work-group Time-Analysis Worksheet that your colleagues complete individually and anonymously.

Be sure that the worksheet categories include informal, as well as formal, activities. One way to generate a comprehensive pool of tasks is to ask colleagues to suggest categories that emerged from their own individual analyses.

OPERATIONAL PRIORITIES AS PROBLEM-DEFINERS

Charles Kepner and Benjamin Tregoe have observed that a problem is the deviation between what is and what ought to be. Operational priorities are the "is" of a situation. Time analysis, for example, is a way to measure operational priorities.

Theoretical priorities are the "ought" of a situation. Job-performance objectives, for example, are indicators of theoretical priorities. Once I know the operational priorities for my work group and/or myself, I can compare this information to the data I collected about my theoretical priorities. The gap, if any, between my operational priorities and my theoretical priorities defines my disorganization problem. Comparing the "is" with the "ought" describes the level of disorganization in the situation.

Once a problem of priority disorganization has been defined, then there are several approaches a manager may use to solve that problem. These approaches are geared toward closing the gap between is and ought. In the next chapter, I shall discuss these approaches.

THE MAIN POINT

Your operational priorities are your use of time. To be an effective manager, you must know what your operational priorities are—not only what you wish them to be, or believe them to be, but what they actually are as measured by what you do with your time over any given period. Time analysis is a measure of your operational priorities. Time logs do not solve problems. They simply serve to help you to identify problems more accurately.

CHAPTER 4

The Problem of Priority Dissonance

Functioning organizations require functional organizing systems. Unfortunately, "dysfunctioning" systems rather than "functioning" systems are the norm for many work groups and individuals.

Dysfunctional organizing systems emerge when a gap develops between what I say I wish to do and what I actually do. I call this gap "priority dissonance." Priority dissonance is the disparity, if any, between a system's operational and theoretical priorities.

This disparity is at the heart of many organizing problems. My organizing systems cannot be completely functional when the arrangements I make to support what I'm doing are inconsistent with the arrangements I need to support what I wish to do. When priority dissonance emerges in my life, I am, literally, organizing against myself.

WHY DOES IT HAPPEN?

Priority dissonance occurs when I find myself in the position of wanting one thing but doing something else. Priority dissonance doesn't make any sense, and because it makes no sense, it places my telic nature under a great deal of pressure. So why would I, or any other healthy human system, allow such a senseless condition to emerge?

I believe that most of us get into the bind of priority dissonance because we do not fully understand what we are doing to ourselves when we talk about or think about what we wish to do or be. To put it bluntly, we have no idea what we are doing to our heads when we open our mouths.

Now a lot of very fascinating and very complex theories from cognitive and physiological psychology are available that offer some insight into this area. These theories explain how the brain works and the relationships between thought and behavior. However, rather than plunge into a treatise on these theories (a treatise that would definitely tax the ability of the writer if not the interest of the reader), I would like to offer a fable about how a case of priority dissonance emerged in my own life.

I shall relate the tale in terms I have created to help myself and others understand what happens in our heads when we say one thing and do another. This story, while it is based on my understanding of scientific theories, is not in itself scientific. Rather, it may be regarded as allegorical, a symbolic narration of the calamity of priority dissonance that endangers "everyman" and "everywoman."

THE STORY OF THE GYM, THE POPCORN, AND THE PAPERBACK THRILLERS

A while back, I went through the "One-Hundred-Years Old" exercise as a way to review my life goals. A new and interesting personal value emerged: I wanted to be not only healthy, but gorgeous, at sixty-five.

Now I realized almost immediately that if I were going to come even close to my vision of being a senior-citizen beauty queen, I needed to start working on a few things right away. A primary objective was to shape up the old body. So I established the six-month goal of joining and attending a health club.

Recognizing the unpredictable nature of my professional schedule, I didn't sign up for any specific exercise class but joined the club on a "drop-in" basis. So I wrote the goal: "I go to the health club and exercise whenever my schedule permits for at least one hour, at least four times a week, for a period of six months."

I was very pleased with this goal. I was so pleased I talked about it every chance I got. I told my family about it. I told my friends about it. I told colleagues and even chance acquaintances about it: "Well, I'm really committed to physical fitness. I go to the gym at least four times a week."

Now what was I really doing with all this talk? Well, I was "psyching myself up." I was trying to get my brain ready to order my body to actually go and do all that work when a free hour arose. And in fact, my brain was getting ready.

You see, our brains want to take care of us. Richard Restak, author of *The Brain*, has described the brain as a practical organ, designed for the purpose of bringing about changes in the environment. The brain structures and restructures itself to enable us to get things done. What things? Whatever we tell it to do.

So let's imagine that when I went around stating that I believed in exercise and that I wanted to exercise, my brain, good friend to me that it is, restructured itself to be ready to take me to the health club. This restructuring involved the creation of what I call "readiness pathways."

Readiness pathways may be regarded as assemblages of potential behaviors, behaviors that need to be available to me if I am going to achieve a desired goal. In this case, readiness pathways emerged to get me to the gym (pack gym bag, carry membership card, drive car along correct route) as a result of my saying I wanted to go to the health club. Put another way, hearing what I wanted to do, my brain got ready to help me do it.

So I was ready to go to the gym whenever I was

free for at least an hour, a minimum of four times a week, for six months. However, about a month and a half into this six-month plan, it started to occur to me that something was very wrong.

The problem began in the second week. A clear and cold evening in November, I had completed the day's work and even had things pretty well set up for the next day. My husband and son had gone out to a chess club meeting. This evening was truly time for me, a perfect opportunity to go to the gym.

But did I allow my brain to activate those readiness pathways and order my body to pack my gym bag, get my membership card, take the car out of the garage, drive to the health club, and work out? No. Instead, I ordered my brain to make my body go into the kitchen, pop some popcorn, go to my son's room, pick out a paperback thriller from the stack he had read, go back to the living room, curl up on the couch, and cool out.

Now what kind of restructuring can we imagine goes on in the brain this time? Well, first I would suppose that the readiness pathways for exercising receive a bit of a jolt. All the cues they had been getting from the environment (free time, car available, gym clothes clean) had been signaling "go." However, the actual command, when it came, was "stop."

Second, we can imagine that another kind of pathway was created to enable me to pop the popcorn, get the book, and lie down. I call these pathways "necessary pathways."

69

Necessary pathways may be regarded as patterns of actual behaviors. The first time an order is sent "to do something right now," a necessary pathway is forged. The more often the behavior is repeated, the deeper, or more "channelized," the pathway becomes. So we can imagine that every time I order my body to do something new or unexpected, the brain, practical organ that it is, creates structures that not only allow me to complete an activity in the present but also make it easier for me to repeat that activity in the future.

And this, indeed, is what happened. As the weeks went by, I found it easier and easier to repeat the popcorn–book–lie down–cool out activity during periods of free time. The necessary pathways for this activity became deeper and deeper. Meanwhile, however, I continued to verbalize my high regard for physical fitness and my commitment to exercising at the gym four times a week. The readiness pathways were also constantly being recharged.

The idea I am attempting to suggest here is that we can restructure our brain in two ways:

1. We may restructure our brains through our intentions—what we wish to do, our theoretical priorities. Our theoretical priorities create readiness pathways.

2. We may also restructure our brains through our physical behaviors—what we actually do, our operational priorities. Our operational priorities create necessary pathways.

When these restructurings are at cross-purposes, when the established pathways run in opposing directions, a tremendous strain is placed on the human system. As one social commentator has observed, "There is nothing more painful, more productive of anxiety, depression, and despair, than not being able to succeed in a task that has deep psychological significance for oneself."

Through the establishment of readiness pathways, exercising took on a deep psychological significance for me. Through the establishment of opposing necessary pathways, however, it became less and less likely that I would succeed at exercising. And the outcome of this inconsistency was increasing feelings of discomfort and unease.

Now it's important to note that I did not feel any guilt or anxiety the first time I engaged in the popcorn–book–lie down–cool out behavior. I was entitled to a break, I told myself. I had worked very hard that day, and besides, I'd been to the gym five times the previous week.

But as I engaged in this behavior more frequently, its necessary pathways became more channelized and more clearly in conflict with the readiness pathways for exercising. I had constructed a conflicting structure of pathways. And I was beginning to feel slightly crazy about the whole matter.

By the third month of my so-called exercise program, I had restructured myself into a mess. Why? Because I wasn't paying attention to the consistency (or inconsistency) of the structures I was creating. I had forgotten the importance of that most simple, almost simplistic, of organizing adages, Organizing Adage 6:

> Your brain hears
> what your mouth says.

GETTING RID OF PRIORITY DISSONANCE

Priority dissonance is the gap between what you are doing and what you say you wish to do. Closing the gap eliminates the dissonance. And how do you close the gap?

The gap of priority dissonance can be closed in one of two ways:

1. I can go to the gym four times a week.

or

2. I can establish the goal of cooling out as one means of ensuring that I have a less wrinkled brow when I'm sixty-five. In addition, I can drop the goal of going to the health club four times a week.

In short, I can change my behavior, or I can change my goals.

Changing Behavior

For decades, psychologists have been studying how and why human beings change behavior. From these studies, a wealth of "behavior-modification" techniques have emerged—among them things known as "feedback charts," "reward schedules," "visualizations," and "affirmations." These approaches have been used by a wide assortment of people interested in changing behavior, from Weight Watchers to the New York Jets.

Affirmations, for example, are written statements about one's self intended to formalize a personal goal. They have been widely used in sports psychology and represent a simple, yet powerful technique for changing behavior. Laurie Handlers, a Washington, D.C.-based consultant specializing in affirmation and visualization training, constantly emphasizes the high suggestibility of the sub-conscious and the power this suggestibility has over our behavior. "Affirmations are simple," Ms. Handlers observes, "but their power is frequently misunderstood because they are so simple."

When constructing an affirmation, make sure your statement is positive, personal, and in the present tense, such as:

- "I swim thirty laps in twenty minutes."

- "I limit all my committee meetings to sixty minutes or less."

- "I contact at least fifty prospective clients every week."

If you decide to deal with priority dissonance by modifying your behavior through affirmations, be sure to:

73

1. Write each affirmation on a separate index card or sheet of paper.

2. Read the affirmation aloud to yourself at least three times a day for at least twenty-one days. (A lot of psychological research seems to support the notion that *twenty-one* is the magic number for behavior change and habit formation.)

Although your affirmation may not be true when you write it, a conscious, systematic program of deepening your "readiness pathways" increases pressure on your body to act. Every behavior in the direction of the affirmation releases some of the pressure and strengthens the related "necessary pathways"—that is, your ability to elicit the behavior again.

With affirmations, you use the relationship between your brain and your mouth as a means to get what you want instead of a means to make yourself crazy. Over time, behavior meshes more and more closely with affirmation, and you're off and running (or swimming, as the case may be).

Changing Goals

Although we hear a lot about the power we have to change what we do, we hear little about the power we have to change what we want. I don't have to become vice-president of human and organizational development by the time I'm forty-five. I don't have to double the dollar value of my sales this year. I don't even have to exercise four times a week.

What I do "have to do" is to be consistent with my own values. But the same value can be supported by many different goals.

Therefore, the second method I have at my disposal for removing priority dissonance suggests that I:

1. Determine what value (or values) the troublesome goal is serving.

2. Decide if that value (or values) is still important to me.

3. If so, establish another set of goals that are not only consistent with the value (or values) in question but also consistent with my present patterns of behavior (my operational priorities) and thereby let myself off the hook.

4. If not, forget the whole thing and thereby let myself off the hook.

For example, to resolve the priority dissonance in my allegorical tale, I can set up a behavior-modification program that would induce me to get to the gym four times a week. However, I can also reevaluate the goal of going to the gym at all:

• What value does this goal support? This goal supports the value of "physical beauty in old age."

• Is this value still important to me? Well, yes.

- Besides going to the health club four times a week, what other activities might support this value? Well, several come to mind:

  1. Go to the gym three times a week.
  2. Do calisthenics at home four times a week.
  3. Buy an exercise bike and pedal while reading the thriller.
  4. Define "physical beauty in old age" as "an unworried brow in a mature body."

- Which activities are most consistent with what I am already doing? Activities 2, 3, and 4.

- Which goal shall I establish for the next six months? I'll start with activity 2. If, upon a three-week evaluation, I see that that is not working out, I shall go to 3. (This goal also aids me by cutting down on popcorn consumption, since it's difficult to munch, peddle, and read at the same time.) I'll hold "activity" 4 in reserve as a last resort.

Changing Goals Is Not Copping Out

Changing goals is an effective way to eliminate priority dissonance. But some of you at this point may be thinking that changing goals is really copping out, giving up. I would like to suggest that it is not.

Remember that we are purposeful beings. Whatever activities we are engaged in, we are engaged in them for some reason. If we look at our operational priorities as "goals in action," we can see that, in many cases, our telic natures have already "changed" goals for us through the actual behaviors that we perform. Changing our statements of purpose (theoretical priorities) is simply a conscious acknowledgment of goal changes that have already taken place. We're not copping out. We're just owning up and getting on with it.

PRIORITY DISSONANCE AND PROCRASTINATION

An interesting connection exists between priority dissonance and procrastination. Since priority dissonance is the gap between what I wish to do and what I'm doing, and procrastination is saying I want to do something but not doing it, we can view procrastination as a special case of priority dissonance.

The most frequently recommended remedies for procrastination involve modifying behavior. This approach assumes that I really understand and want those goals I'm procrastinating over. All I need are some "motivators" and "reinforcements" to get started.

But as with priority dissonance in general, there are two options for dealing with procrastination. Yes, I can modify my behavior to meet my goals. But I also have the option of questioning and reevaluating my goals.

The truth is that frequently we say we want to do things we really don't want to do at all. Rather, outside forces (our parents, our culture, our neighbors, our boss) have instructed us that we "should" want them. "I should shoot for that promotion." "I should send Christmas cards." "I should plant flowers out by the mailbox."

We may have no clear idea if or how these "should" activities connect to our value system. So since we don't understand them, we resist doing them. We procrastinate.

For example, it could be that I never really wanted to drag out to a health club four times a week. Maybe I bought a whole lot of "shoulds" concerning fancy exercise equipment, elegant "workout" togs, and handsome weight machine instructors.

In fact, I didn't want any of this. What I really wanted was to put on my old gray sweatsuit from my college PE days, do twenty minutes of old-fashioned calisthenics on the living room floor, run in place for five minutes, and be done with it. Procrastination was a way for my brain to try to take care of me (again). By putting off going to the health club, it was saying:

> "I'm not really ready to have you do this yet. Oh, I know you keep saying, 'I go to the health club four times a week.' But the readiness pathways have remained pretty shallow. I'm not convinced this is something you really want to do. Before you plunk down another hundred bucks for a quarterly membership, maybe you should reevaluate whether going to the health club is a goal you really want."

On the other hand, if I do decide my goals are OK and therefore resolve to change my behavior, feedback charts and reward schedules can be effective tools to ward off procrastination. Especially with long-term and difficult objectives, a system of periodic feedback and rewards is necessary to get the impetus up and keep it going.

However, be sure to reward yourself for the right activities. When an organizing system involves arrangements that reward me for working toward one set of goals and not another, I will put off working on the "unrewarded" goals. I may find myself working on less important but rewarded things and postponing work on more important but unrewarded things. I'll be right back to procrastinating again.

THE MAIN POINT

Earlier in this book, I defined an effective organizing system as arrangements of people, paper, physical objects, space, and priorities that support your goals and objectives. These arrangements are the result of behaviors you engage in each day. If your behaviors (operational priorities) are inconsistent with your stated goals (theoretical priorities), then your arrangements are inconsistent with your goals, and your organizing system is dysfunctional.

Priority dissonance, therefore, is a sign of a dysfunctional organizing system. The correction for dysfunction is the same for individuals and for work groups: either change your behavior (that is, your arrangements of people, paper, physical objects, space, and priorities) so it is consistent with your stated goals, or change your stated goals so they are consistent with the arrangements you have made.

You may choose either one. But you must confront the problem of priority dissonance if you are to achieve effective organizing systems for yourself and for your organization.

CHAPTER 5

Organizing for Competing Goals, or "Keeping Peace in the Pantheon"

Organizing is a process. It is a process centered around our values and goals. When we organize, we make arrangements of people, paper, space, physical objects, and time in order to operationalize certain values by achieving certain goals.

We each have values that reflect the multiple aspects of our lives. For example, we have personal values. These values relate primarily to our wishes for personal well-being. In addition, we have values that relate to a sense of family and family life. And finally, we have professional values, beliefs, and desires concerning work and working. Each set of values implies a corresponding set of goals.

Sometimes we are able to organize our lives so that the arrangements we make for one set of goals are also supportive of another set of goals. For instance, the value of "expertness: becoming an authority" may be very important to me right now. I may set the professional goal of delivering at least four talks within the next year.

In addition to expertness, I may hold in high esteem the value of "affection: obtaining and sharing companionship." To operationalize that value, I may set a one-year personal goal of meeting at least three persons of the opposite sex with whom I feel relaxed and compatible, with the two-year personal goal of marriage.

Now I may be able to make arrangements that address both. If I am able to expand my social circle while also being a guest speaker (for example, attending a luncheon or dinner with the sponsors prior to the talk or, better yet, attending a cocktail party offered by the sponsors after the talk!), then I can fulfill professional values and personal values, both at the same time.

More often than not, however, we find that by making the arrangements needed to achieve one set of goals, we are excluded from making the arrangements to achieve another set of goals. If the den is arranged as a computer center (supportive of a professional goal), it cannot also be arranged as a billiards room (supportive of a family goal). If my boss asks me whether I would like to make the department's presentation to the executive planning committee Wednesday evening and I say yes (related to a professional goal), then I shall be unable to make a presentation to my community

planning board, also meeting Wednesday evening
(and related to a personal goal).

Now I really want and value both of these goals.
I want to position myself for a substantial promotion by May. I want the town to install bike trails
by June. So this situation is not a problem of priority dissonance. The problem here is one of priority
competition.

I want to "get it all together," but pieces of my
organizing system keep "coming apart": competing demands for time, competing demands for
space, competing demands for physical and financial resources. How is "organizing" humanly possible with all of this going on?

GOALS AS "GODS AND GODDESSES"

The fates often seem dead set against organizing.
In fact, I would like to suggest that one way to
get a handle on what is happening when our goals
clash (and what, maybe, we can do about it)
is to think of goals and values as "gods and goddesses."

David Miller, psychologist and theologian, suggests that values are deities, gods and goddesses,
that are at the core of the goals of our lives. He
comments, "The gods and goddesses are worlds
of being and meaning in which my personal life
participates."

If we think about how we frequently refer to
values, we can intuitively accept Miller's meta-

phor. Sometimes we describe a person as one who "worships fame" (the value of prestige), or "worships money" (the value of wealth), or "worships his wife" (the value of affection). What do we mean? Well, what we mean is that these values (prestige, money, affection) are the primary shapers of this person's goals. The person in question organizes to achieve goals that actualize these values.

As I pointed out at the beginning of this chapter, each of us holds multiple types of goals. These goals represent various value centers, or deities. I have professional goals, family goals, personal goals—all of which support an assortment of deities, or values (in my case, leadership, affection, and service).

I am, in short, a veritable walking pantheon. Miller refers to this as "polytheism of the psyche": many potencies, many structures of meaning, all present in the reality of our everyday lives. These multiple meanings, or deities, exist simultaneously. And more often than not, they seem to be at war with one another for elevation to the center of our organizing stage.

This warfare is usually frustrating, often angering. I need (want) all of my value centers. All of the deities require acknowledgment and homage. Yet one or the other always seems to be trying to squeeze the rest out.

In my anger and frustration, I usually do one of two things:

1. Attempt a conversion to "monotheism"—
   that is, I try to get all my values together in
   one neat package.

   or

2. Attempt to banish one or more of the deities
   to the wilderness.

However, gods and goddesses cannot be dealt
with so cavalierly. They resist losing their individual identities in a consolidation move. And
they certainly balk at being cast out altogether. In
fact, whenever I take either of these approaches
to competing goals, I only make matters worse.

THE PROBLEM WITH
"GETTING IT ALL TOGETHER"

For many of us, "being organized" has meant "getting it all together." A truly organized person
(so we've been told) is not tripped up by competing
demands on his or her resources. Rather, the
truly organized person makes arrangements that
take care of everything, somehow. This mythical
paragon of organizing is frequently described as
"knowing what he or she wants and going for it,"
"focused," "consistent."
In short, we are told that the best way to deal
with the strains of polytheism is to convert to
monotheism: take all the gods and goddesses that

represent the pantheon of your goals and collapse them together into a monolithic paramount deity. The monotheistic ideal is to create one organizing system—that is, make one set of arrangements—that takes care of everything: all of my values, all of my goals. Then I can appear "focused." Then I can "look like I know what I'm doing."

Thus, the "monotheistic ideal" emphasizes consistency: somehow I should design one organizing system in my life—one arrangement of people, paper, space, physical objects, and time—that supports all my goals and all my values. Then, I should consistently use this one system to get things done. To follow the "monotheistic ideal," for example, I would design a time schedule that took into account as many of my values as possible, and then I would stick with it. I would "always" review the consulting schedule between 7:30 and 8:00 A.M. I would "always" exercise on Monday, Wednesday, and Friday lunch hours. I would "always" go out to dinner with my family on Wednesday nights.

In real life, however, it is virtually impossible to achieve this monotheistic ideal. There is always one or another recalcitrant god or goddess, one or another value center, that simply refuses to fit into some master organizing system. The problem with this approach is that an emphasis on consistency sucks us into what psychologist Kenneth Gergen refers to as the "fallacy of a monolateral identity." Just because I have chosen this one arrangement of time as a way to meet my goals, I begin to believe it is the only arrangement of time I can or should make. I come to believe that I have, and that it is desirable to have, a single, stable, consistent identity: "Jane, who reviews the consulting schedule between 7:30 and 8:00 A.M.; exercises at lunch hour every Monday, Wednesday, and Friday; and takes her family out to dinner on Wednesday nights." Somehow, I come to identify this kind of "monolateral" behavior with "being organized."

In fact, however, my identity and the organizing system that supports it, must be changeable. I need to be able to change because lots of different gods and goddesses go in and out of my pantheon all the time. As Gergen puts it, "The healthy, happy human being wears many masks." When different deities (value centers) emerge in my life, I need to be able to change masks (identities) and change my organizing arrangements to support them.

No single identity can possibly take in all of the gods and goddesses that play through my life. No fixed pattern of organizing arrangements can possibly encompass them all. But (as I shall elaborate on below) woe unto me if I try to leave any of the deities out.

So attempts at "monotheistic" organizing are really of little help in dealing with the question of competing goals. Monotheistic organizing is of no help because (1) it falsely leads us into thinking that we could acknowledge all of our value centers with one set of arrangements; and (2) it locks us into a "monolateral identity," an identity that thwarts the flexibility we need in order to pay homage to each of our value centers.

Monotheistic organizing doesn't work. Through bitter experience, most of us know it doesn't work. Yet we still struggle for this ideal, the ideal of "getting it all together." And in doing so, we tangle ourselves up in a second approach that doesn't work either: attempting to banish recalcitrant deities to the wilderness.

STIRRING UP THE FURIES

"The Powers that are fundamental to our very being are in contention." So observes David Miller. And how well we know it. The very values that define and direct my telic nature sometimes seem to be engaged in a Trojan War that threatens to tear that very nature apart.

I want to fulfill a number of purposes in my life. Yet at any given moment, my own purposes frequently seem to be at cross-purposes! If I'm here, I can't be there. If I'm doing this, I can't do that. Oh, I attempt to pursue the "monotheistic ideal" by establishing goals that support many of my values. But there always seems to be at least one value, one god or goddess, that just doesn't fit into the arrangement of things at the moment.

Now having a deity or two hanging around loose at the edges (that is, a value that refuses to blend in with the overall monolithic arrangement of things) makes a monotheist very nervous. So what do I do?

Well, I attempt to ignore or even deny the existence of deities (values) that I can't seem to pay homage to (that is, can't seem to achieve). I find myself saying things like: "True, I can't seem to fit in taking those banking courses I'd need to be in line for that new job coming up. But you know, getting *that* promotion wouldn't make that much difference in my money situation, anyway." Or, "Well, I haven't had time to play the piano much lately, but my music is just a hobby." Or, "We want to have kids, but we don't see how we can fit it into our professional and financial plans. Besides, it's a crime to bring children into a world like this anyway."

The question I would like to raise with you is this: what does a god or goddess do when we attempt to banish him or her to the wilderness? What happens when we attempt to deny the existence of something that is truly important to us?

Well, the Greeks, who had plenty of experience dealing with gods and goddesses, had a story to describe what happens. According to this story, a heavenly wedding was announced. A handsome god and a beautiful goddess (the daughter of a very powerful god) were to be united in a gala celebration. Everyone was to be invited. Everyone, that is, except three goddess sisters. These sisters were rather ugly, and it was felt that they wouldn't "fit" into the beautiful arrangements that were being made. So the bride's father simply "forgot" to invite them.

On the day of the wedding, all hell broke loose. The sisters showed up anyway and vented a havoc that was awesome to behold. The wine was soured. Winds and rains destroyed all the beautiful "arrangements" of flowers, canopies, and so on. Even the nuptial bed was befouled with grit and sand.

But the sisters didn't stop at the wedding. They continued to play havoc with the lives of the unfortunate couple and all those who had attempted to ignore the existence of the misfits. The sisters whirled and swirled through the lives of their offenders, disorganizing those lives wherever they went. The sisters came to be called "the Furies."

SO WHAT IS TO BE DONE?

Just looking at the broad areas of our personal, professional, and family value centers, it is simply not in the nature of human systems that all of our goals will harmoniously fit together all the time. Take the area of work, for example. Albert Rice and Eric Miller, in their book *Systems of Organization*, explain the principle clearly:

> Except in very primitive communities in which work, play and family life are all integrated community activities, the members of an enterprise carry within themselves memberships of many different groups with many different activity systems. However positively they accept the definition and methods of performance of an enterprise's primary task, it is unlikely that values derived from all their other different memberships will

always be in harmony with those attached to work. [p. 29]

There is usually some value that doesn't fit in. But just because a value doesn't fit in, that doesn't mean that I can shut it out. If I try to do that, that value is liable to become "furious." So what can I do? How can I organize arrangements for competing goals?

Again, guidance may come from looking back to those master mediators of polytheistic competition, the Greeks. Let's return to the wedding story.

After a long period of turmoil, it occurred to someone in the cosmos that the Furies were stirring up so much trouble because they wanted attention. They were all over the place because nobody had acknowledged that they had a right to any place. They were goddesses, value centers. They deserved homage. And yet they had been ignored.

And so the harassed newlyweds arranged for a temple to be built for the Furies on Mt. Olympus. Here they would have "a place." Here they would be acknowledged. And here (although they still might not be invited to all the social occasions— after all, they were still ugly) they would have their own festival days on which they would receive homage and recognition.

The Furies moved into their home. They received homage in their "time and place," accepting that there were times and places where they just didn't fit in. And things calmed down.

91

Now what does this story suggest concerning our own organizing strategies? Well, first we should become actively "polytheistic" in our organizing. We should actively and openly acknowledge each of our value centers. We should give each value center or cluster of value centers (the three sisters—that is, related values) a "place" in our scheme of things, no matter how "inconsistent" it is with the other deities in our lives. We should then arrange to let our deities know that we realize they're there, although they may not be at the center of our arrangement at the moment.

In short, instead of trying to "get it all together" (the "it" being the values in our lives), we should organize our lives to "keep it all apart." By consciously acknowledging, and assigning a place to, each of our value centers, we are less likely to "forget" any of them. And we are less likely to stir up the "furious" competition we most dread.

Put another way, if we really want to have all the goals in our lives come together in harmony, we have to consciously keep them apart. We have to organize "polytheistically." As James Hillman, another Jungian psychologist, comments in the book *Jung's Topology*, "without a consciously polytheistic psychology we are more susceptible to an unconscious fragmentation. . . . "

Which brings us to Organizing Adage 7:

**To get it all together,
acknowledge that it's all apart.**

THE ART OF "POLYTHEISTIC ORGANIZING"

Most of us are products of a monotheistic culture. Therefore, we don't know what to do with a whole bunch of gods and goddesses, especially when they get into contention. What we usually do is try to blend them all together and/or bump off the recalcitrants.

I have tried to suggest that our monotheistic world view may actually exacerbate some of the organizing problems it is meant to solve. If we organize with rather than against our multivalue reality, we are way ahead of the game.

Continuing to draw on our mythological metaphor, polytheism is not the act of paying homage to all our value centers at once. Polytheism is the act of acknowledging that many value centers exist; that they are separate, discrete entities; and that we pay attention to them *one at a time.*

Polytheism is, in this sense, "consecutive monotheisms." It is a way of looking at ourselves that allows for multiple meanings to exist simultaneously, yet for each meaning to be acted on individually. As David Miller puts it: "One god at a time. In [my] time, many gods."

Polytheistic organizing involves:

1. Constructing a pantheon for my value centers and making sure that each value center has a place.

2. Paying homage (that is, paying attention) to

93

one value center or cluster of value centers at a time.

3. Over time, paying homage to each value center.

First, how do you "construct a pantheon"? Well, my suggestion will sound so simple (maybe even simplistic after the high-level journey we've just taken through mythology and psychology) that some of you may laugh out loud upon reading it. I would like to propose that we construct a pantheon for our values when we explicitly *identify our theoretical goals by category* (for example, personal, professional, and family) and then *write them down.*

Now you may understand why I emphasized categorizing your values in chapter 2. By establishing categories, you create a place for each of the deities in your life.

Moreover, now it may make sense to you why every goal-setting program everywhere tells you to write your goals down. By writing each goal down, you acknowledge each one. And every time you reread your goals, you reaffirm each one. If you don't write down your goals, the tendency will be for some of them to be lost sight of in the competition for your time and attention. When these deities get shoved aside, you may find yourself acting increasingly disorganized on the outside and feeling increasingly "furious" on the inside.

The second and third aspects of polytheistic organizing propose that we pay attention to one value center or cluster of value centers at a time, while over time, paying attention to each value center. The question then arises, "How will I know which value center to pay attention to when, especially when they seem to be competing?" My suggestions here are a bit less simple and, I'm afraid, to some of you will seem much less concrete.

I would like to suggest that, while setting goals is a logical, "left-brain" activity, choosing which goal to pursue when is an intuitive, "right-brain" activity. In fact, in the latter case, we are most effective not when we choose the goals but when we let the goals choose us.

In the language of our polytheistic metaphor, the gods and goddesses in any pantheon come in and out of ascendancy. At any given time, one or another of them will let me clearly know that he or she or they represent the important value center to organize my life around right now. Even when there appear to be competing demands for my time, I can usually "sense," if I don't think about it too much, what my ascendant value is right now.

It may be difficult for me to tell my child that, right now, my ascendant value is professional—specifically, to get the promotion that's coming up—and that I therefore have to go to the board meeting tonight and will not be attending his or her play. It may be difficult to say those words, but in my heart of hearts, it is not difficult to "know" that they are true. (If you want to imagine another "difficulty," imagine the opposite situation: I "know" that my family values are the most important to me right now, and I've got to decline the boss's invitation to attend the meeting!)

However, real battles for ascendancy do erupt in the pantheon. They tend to erupt when a new cluster of deities is rising to ascendancy and the dominant cluster of deities (with their related organizing arrangements) doesn't want to acquiesce.

Based on information and resources available in the environment, our value centers tend to assert themselves when it's "their turn" in the scheme of things. In the language of our metaphor, we can think of a liturgical calendar that corresponds, for example, to the developmental stages and phases of our lives. As we go through the cycles, different values become important, and different clusters of goals, with their supporting organizing arrangements, should peacefully follow each other in succession.

This view of life, goals, and appropriate goal changing is eloquently suggested in the famous Bible passage: "To everything there is a season, and a time for every *purpose* [emphasis mine] under heaven." There is a time for each of our value centers to have ascendancy, and in time, each can have ascendancy.

However, this is the point where our old bugaboo "consistency" trips us up. As Kenneth Gergen points out, "All of us are burdened by the code of coherence which demands that we ask: 'How can I be X if I really am Y, its opposite?'"

We have a whole set of goals in place, and all the arrangements of people, paper, physical objects, space, and time that go with it. To a great extent, all of this defines who we are. We are loath to acknowledge that it may be time to be "someone else." It may be time to move on to another temple in the pantheon.

We are loath to move on because we're afraid. We're afraid we'll look "inconsistent," as if we "don't know what we're doing": "Well, gee, a couple of years ago Sam was all gung-ho for his kids and family, and now he's spending all his time trying to get to the top of the department. Must be having trouble at home." We're afraid of all the reshuffling of arrangements we'll have to make: "Yes, our focus during the first year was to encourage as much informal interaction as possible among the staff so we could generate a lot of new-product ideas. But now we have to put technical meat onto those ideas. And for that, we need peace and quiet. Therefore, we should either put doors on all the cubicles or convert the lounges into a library/study area." And we're afraid that we'll never get back to the threatened value centers again: "If, in order to push ahead with my professional writing, I drop my exercising, I'll never start exercising again."

The polytheistic approach to organizing encourages us to see that it's OK to change. In fact, it's imperative to change if we want to avoid trouble. These rearrangements do not represent "mistakes" or "wastes of time," but effective organizing processes. In a pantheon, all of the gods and goddesses remain, even when I am not paying attention to them. When it's their turn, they will reassert themselves again.

For example, as long as physical form and fitness remain important to me, that goddess will reside in my pantheon. The ascendancy of the goddesses of creativity and professionalism may have, in their rising, caused me to turn my focus from exercising right now. But the goddess of form and fitness is important to me. I still affirm her as a value center. And therefore, someday, when the signals from the environment are right, she will assert herself again. And if I am sensitive, and if I can let go of whatever deities are dominant at the time, I shall turn again to her.

I believe this concept of "turning" is at the heart of dealing with what appear to be "competing" goals. The Greeks built their pantheons in circular form. If we think of our value centers as formed in a circle, then we can envision "polytheistic organizing" as the process of shifting focus, shifting arrangements, turning from one deity toward another. The outcome, hopefully, is balance and harmony that keep peace in the pantheon. As the old Shaker hymn reflects, "Turning, turning will be our delight till by turning, turning we come 'round right."

IMPLICATIONS FOR THE WORK GROUP

This discussion has focused primarily on our individual organizing processes. In the next chapter, I shall focus on a battle among gods that is endemic to work groups: meetings.

However, the concept of "polytheistic organizing" also has several other implications for work groups. First, work groups should not tangle themselves into inaction by trying to make arrangements that cover everything before they'll use arrangements to cover anything. Flexibility and change are OK. Maybe if we spent less money on our filing systems or space dividers, we'd be more willing to rearrange these elements when our goals changed. Instead, we frequently fight to hold onto obsolete goals because we don't want to be "stuck" with obsolete arrangements.

This point suggests the second implication of the "polytheistic" approach to organizing for work groups. Goals or value centers let us know, through signals from the environment, when it is their time for ascendancy. A work group that strives for "consistency," locking in on one goal or cluster of goals without ever changing focus, does so at its own peril. Work groups can and should change direction, and they should be allowed to modify their organizing arrangements so as to support those changes.

Finally, the concept of "polytheistic organizing" allows you and your work group to really trust that it's OK to work on one thing at a time. You don't have to run around trying to accomplish everything at once just because all of these goals are in your action plans. In time, each of your objectives will come into ascendancy, and then, if you are sensitive and flexible, you will pay attention to it. Which brings me to . . .

THE MAIN POINT

Whether as an individual or as part of a work group, we each have many different types of values. These clusters of goals or value centers may be regarded as gods and goddesses, each of whom requires acknowledgment and homage. If I fail to acknowledge them, they become "furious." My challenge is to give each deity "a place" and to know and accept when it is in ascendancy. Changing focus to acknowledge different value centers may make me appear inconsistent. But that is OK, even necessary. As Walt Whitman asserted: "Do I contradict myself? Very well then, I contradict myself. I am large. I contain multitudes."

CHAPTER 6

The
Meaning of Meetings

Most of us, at some point in our professional lives, have come across at least one book or article or workshop on how to conduct a meeting. Virtually hundreds of such books, articles, and workshops exist.

One example is the "Meeting Bill of Rights," proposed by Dru Scott in her book *How to Put More Time in Your Life*. The "Meeting Bill of Rights" affirms that everyone involved in a meeting is entitled to know in advance (1) the meeting objective, (2) what question the meeting should answer, (3) what each participant is expected to contribute, and (4) what time the meeting will be over.

Although other sources may go into more detail on these points, Scott's work exemplifies the focus of most of what has been written and taught about meetings. This focus is a "how" orientation: how meetings should be conducted.

But relatively little has been said concerning *why* meetings are conducted in the first place. Why do mature, mentally healthy human beings spend so much time getting together in what are frequently poorly ventilated (and/or poorly heated) smoke-filled rooms? What purposes are our telic natures attempting to fulfill when we schedule hours of our time in an activity that few of us understand and most of us say we don't like?

People in organizations hold a lot of formal meetings. It is not unreasonable to estimate that the average white-collar executive will spend approximately thirty thousand hours in meetings during his or her working career. Depending on how you calculate it, this figure represents from one-third to almost one-half of all the working hours for such a person!

Meetings therefore appear to have a very high operational priority in the lives of many people. But what values are being fulfilled, what purposes are being served by all these meetings? I noted earlier that our telic natures rebel against meaningless activity. If we are forced into such activity, we feel "slightly crazy." Is this, maybe, why meetings bother us so much? Do meetings make any sense? Do meetings have any meaning, and if so, what is it?

In this chapter, I would like to suggest first why meetings are such a fact of organizational life.

Then I shall point out two very important organizational values that are served by meetings. Finally, at the end of the chapter, I shall offer a few comments on how we can shape our meetings so that they better serve these values. By better understanding the "why" of meetings, maybe our telic natures will feel less crazy when we find ourselves in such gatherings.

THE "WHY" OF MEETINGS

Meetings fulfill a deep human need. George Kelly, John Dewey, Martin Buber, and other noted commentators on the human condition have observed that face-to-face meetings hold together the world of human reality. Together, people construct languages, value systems, and codes of behavior that define "the world."

Regarding human organizations, the reality of any organization is constructed and validated by its individual members. Coming together, these members define goals, affirm values, and establish, as well as reinforce, systems of behavior.

In other words, meetings provide an opportunity for the formation of the collective structures discussed earlier in this book. Collective structures serve to unite the values and goals of the individuals with each other and with those of the organization. If there were no meetings in the place where I work, few, if any, collective structures would form, and my attachment to my place of work would diminish.

Meetings, and the opportunity they provide for the building of collective structures, are especially important where work is focused around what political theorist Langdon Winner calls "information machines." The American workplace is changing from primarily product-oriented companies to information-oriented institutions. Currently, 85 percent of all jobs in America involve some form of information processing.

As more and more of us spend more of our time with information machines, the danger arises that we shall spend less time with each other. As Winner observes, "Developments like electronic news, education, banking and even work, all available through information machines, create a strong impetus for people to dwell within themselves and not reach out."

Yet members of an organization need to reach out and interact if they are going to construct the commonly supported values, goals, and structures of arrangements needed to define the organization as real to them. Without such interaction, the organization remains a legal fiction in the minds of its employees, a fiction with little claim to productivity or loyalty.

Most of us are aware of the need for human interaction in the workplace. This need is most acute in workplaces dominated by information machines. I find it no accident that most of the complaints I receive about "too many meetings" come from persons working in the "high-tech" or "information" industries.

Workers on the assembly line or at the construction site, even on the department-store floor, don't seem to call as many meetings. They don't call as many meetings because they don't need to schedule formal opportunities to interact. Their workday is filled with interaction. One might say (as some supervisors wryly do) that in these settings, the workday is, in fact, one big meeting!

But for employees in high-tech, the bulk of their work activities involve interaction with machines, not people. Over time, working "alone" can create the illusion that I work in an isolated, self-contained world. My conception of "the organization" becomes paler and paler. My connection to the organization becomes weaker and weaker.

At some level, managers sense the need for interaction among work-team members. And so they address this need in the only way they know how: they call a lot of meetings.

A good example of this syndrome came to my attention when I was conducting an organizational assessment for a division of a major computer firm several years ago. The focus of this division was on planning, finance, and research. Thus, virtually every professional, technician, or manager had a computer terminal at his or her workstation. Electronic mail, on-line data bases, facsimile devices, and "superphones" all combined to make this facility a wonder of the information age.

The assessment design called for the interviewing of thirty middle- and upper-level managers.

From these interviews, as well as other measures subsequently administered, a strong and overriding theme emerged. You guessed it. Excessive meetings.

Meetings accounted for nearly 60 percent of the managers' on-site time. The primary concern here was therefore not the quality of the meetings—that is, how effectively they were run. The primary concern was the quantity of meetings—why they were having so many meetings in the first place. As one participant quipped, "It's hard to juggle the time in meetings with the time to do the stuff that's decided in meetings, if anything."

Now it's interesting to note that in most cases of "excessive meetings," the very same people who are complaining about the number of meetings are also the people who are calling meetings. So it was in this case. Upon exploring the "why" of the meetings, nearly every participant discovered that the usual reason he or she called a meeting was for "buy in."

Buy in was a term used in this firm to describe the process of getting as many people as possible involved in every decision. A high value was placed on "buy in" in this division. When we explored the "why" of this value priority, we found that many staff members were very concerned that, given the intrinsically isolated nature of their jobs, they could easily fall into making completely unilateral decisions. Unilateral decisions troubled the managers not only because such decisions would probably be based on too narrow a body of information but also because unilateral decisions carried unilateral responsibility if the decisions went wrong.

Moreover, by calling meetings, ostensibly for "buy in," people got a chance to chat with their colleagues and find out what was going on. They couldn't do this poring over data at their workstations, and the culture of the firm frowned on drop-in office visits.

So the problem of excessive meetings masked two other, more fundamental, problems: (1) managers' reluctance to take responsibility for unilateral decisions and (2) everyone's need to get together. By bringing the work team's values to the surface, we also developed ways to address these problems. First, the awesome telecommunications equipment at their disposal could be used to get "buy in" on decisions without calling a meeting. In fact, sending requests for comments and suggestions over the terminals gave the recipients of those requests more time to reflect on the response. This, in turn, would provide a higher level of feedback than ideas thought up on the spur of the moment at a meeting.

But what about the need to "get together"? Well, the suggestion arose to schedule monthly staff birthday parties and seasonal department or sectionwide lunches as a way to get together. The groups had never had time for such "social amenities" before: they were too busy going to meetings.

Finally, division members acknowledged that some decisions were most efficiently made unilaterally. Staff members gave each other permission to make some decisions on their own. They dealt with the need to take individual responsibility in some cases and to avoid dumping on a person if things went wrong.

WEDDING THE VALUES OF ACTION AND RELATING

Action and relating are two values essential to organizational effectiveness. Every organization must get things done—hopefully, things that support its values and goals. In addition, every organization must provide opportunities for its members to relate to one another. Through these relationships, common meanings, understandings, and systems are constructed that define and validate the reality of the organization for its members.

Both the god of action and the goddess of relating are served by meetings. Meetings give us an opportunity to get things done and interact all at the same time. Unfortunately, this wedded pair is almost always battling. At any given meeting, the action faction angrily tries to get things going while the relating coalition stubbornly holds to getting people (or at least their ideas and values) together.

The opposing goals of "hanging out" versus "getting on with it" are in almost constant contention for ascendancy at meetings. However, I would like to suggest that good meetings, like good marriages, are achieved by maintaining a dialectical balance, a unity of opposites. In this unity, each partner maintains the distinctive attributes that are his or her strong points, at the same time melding with the strong points of the other for the greater enhancement of both.

The god of action is goal-oriented. When he is in a balanced state, he contributes the very desirable quality of decisiveness to meetings. The goddess of relating is process-oriented. When she is in a balanced state, she contributes the very desirable quality of sensitivity to meetings. Thus, when the couple is in harmony, a meeting flows smoothly, with decisiveness and sensitivity. A wonderful experience.

However, when either action or relating pushes for ascendancy (that is, pushes to take over the meeting), it also pushes the pair into imbalance. And the experience of the meeting, like the experience of being a part in any marital dispute, is uncomfortable, to say the least.

When the god of action takes over in a meeting, people feel bulldozed. Decisions get pushed to premature closure. Participants become resentful, distant, and resistant to implementing any solutions that have been "agreed" upon.

On the other hand, when the goddess of relating takes over a meeting, people feel bored. Discussions dwell on feelings, attitudes, and beliefs. Few decisions are made. Participants feel aimless and frustrated.

What steps, then, can we take to keep action and relating in harmony and avoid imbalances in our meetings?

SOME MARRIAGE COUNSELING FOR MEETINGS

Meetings can be improved by recognizing imbalances in action or relating when they occur and correcting them. I would suggest that the best way to balance the god of action when he gets out of hand is to structure meetings for effective relating. And the best way to balance the goddess of relating when she gets out of hand is to structure meetings for effective action.

First, to structure a meeting for effective relating:

1. Draw out the silent members of the group. Ask for their opinions, not facts. Asking for facts may simply put them on the spot.

2. Control the garrulous. When someone rambles on, pick up a phrase he or she utters as an excuse for cutting in and offer the phrase to someone else with a "What are your thoughts on that?"

3. Protect the weak. Commend contributions from junior members of the team.

4. Encourage the clash of ideas. (But discourage the clash of personalities.)

5. Avoid the "suggestion-squashing" reflex. One

problem with suggestions in meetings is that they are easier to ridicule than facts or opinions. So take special note and show special warmth when anyone makes a suggestion. Pick out the best parts of suggestions and get other members to help build them into something that might work. Finally, if another member of the meeting shows the squashing reflex, ask the squasher to produce a better suggestion.

Second, to structure a meeting for effective action:

1. Appoint a timekeeper to clearly announce when the meeting time is one-half elapsed, three-quarters elapsed, and five minutes from its scheduled ending time.

2. Clearly state the purpose of the meeting at its start. Meetings are held for the following purposes:
   - Decision making
   - Recommendations
   - Preliminary deliberations
   - Approval
   - Information sharing

3. At the close of the meeting, make a summary statement of what was agreed upon. Have this statement appear in the minutes. Include the names of persons responsible for future action.

4. Conduct a two-week experiment in "meeting control and cost reduction":

- Reduce all meetings to one-half their normally scheduled time.

- Prohibit the scheduling of back-to-back meetings. Everyone must have at least thirty minutes between meetings.

- Allow anyone who wishes to leave a meeting to do so, without penalty, when the timekeeper announces that the scheduled time for the meeting's end has arrived.

- Institute the "ten-minute meeting." Hold it in an area with no chairs. Permit no smoking, drinking, or eating.

At the end of the experiment, you may have reshaped the course of your department's overrelating, underacting meeting behavior. You may also have gotten a lot of people riled up. But as Susan Streeker commented in her article "No more mad meetings," . . . "it's time to rethink the way time, space and money are being sacrificed on the altar of the conference table."

THE MAIN POINT

Meetings can be successfully organized by focusing first, not on how to run the meeting, but rather on why we are calling the meeting to begin with.

Meetings are of importance to organizations because they support the value of action ("getting things done") and the value of relating ("getting together and getting things understood"). The effective meeting is a happy marriage of the two.

WHERE WE'VE BEEN AND WHERE WE'RE GOING

The first six chapters of this book have taken us on a rather extraordinary journey. Exploring concepts in psychology, philosophy, and mythology, we have clearly moved beyond what is usually associated with the term *time management*. Focusing not only on you as an individual but also on you as a work-group member, we have examined both the "how" and the "why" of organizing.

The next three chapters continue our journey into the realm of organizing. These chapters will focus solely on you as an individual. "Visual stressors," "to-do lists," and "planners" are all nuts-and-bolts issues that directly affect individual organizing behavior. In the last chapter, "Organizing the Organization," I will return to the broader focus of the work group to consider why some organizations remain disorganized in spite of heroic individual organizing efforts.

CHAPTER 7

Visual Stressors: Out of Sight, Out of Mind

The wall in back of Sarah's desk was an extraordinary sight. On it hung a huge bulletin board, and on the bulletin board were tacked what appeared to be dozens of pieces of paper. Every piece of paper was attached to the board by cute little enamel tacks that said, "Remember."

Sarah used her car also as a visual memory-jogger. The receipt for her laundry, an extra key to her apartment that she wanted to drop off at her parents', and a pile of old clothes for the Salvation Army all rode around with Sarah in her car. She had them there so she would "remember."

At home, of course, the refrigerator door was covered with lists and pieces of paper, each representing something Sarah was to do. Even more important for Sarah, however, were the various projects she had piled around the living room and

115

on the dining room table. Sarah's reasoning was that if she ever put these things away, she would never do them. So bank statements waiting for balancing, pictures waiting for pasting into picture albums, granny squares waiting for stitching—all these things sat out prominently so that Sarah would "remember."

But Sarah was troubled. More and more things were being "forgotten." They just weren't getting done. She had missed the deadline for enrolling in the employee stock-option program. She had forgotten to fill in the forms (which were hanging from their own "Remember" tack) on time. She had been driving around with the pile of old clothes in the back seat of her car for several weeks. The granny squares had sat in an increasingly dusty jumble in a corner of the living room for over a year.

On several occasions, Sarah had an overwhelming urge to clear off her bulletin board, clean out her car, tidy up her living room. But then panic would set in: "If I put this stuff away, I'll never do it. Out of sight, out of mind." So Sarah continued to look at the stuff, the stuff continued to stare back at Sarah, and less and less got done.

Sarah had fallen victim to a whole array of what I call "visual stressors." Visual stressors are things I must do, or things that represent things I must do, that I tend to look at (1) while I am supposed to be doing something else and (2) many times before I am ready or able to do them. Visual stressors create anxiety. But why? Assuming that I really want to do an activity (no priority dissonance here), why is it that looking at a reminder of it would cause stress?

MENTAL REHEARSAL

Well, the answer again lies in how our brains work. As I pointed out back in chapter 4, your brain is trying to take care of you. It hears what you say you want to do. And it wants to help you do it.

So your brain has set up a number of reminder mechanisms to help you remember to actually do those things. One of these mechanisms involves a sort of "mental rehearsal" of the desired activity every time you see anything that reminds you of it.

For example, let's say I've left a report lying on my desk so I'll remember to proofread the figures one more time before I send it on to the next department. Every time my glance passes over that report, and as long as my glance rests on that report, a message loop is set off and continues in my mind: "Proof the report. Proof the report. Proof the report." Every time I look, my brain gives me a reminder "to do."

Now you're probably wondering at this point, "So what's so terrible about that? Isn't that what you want it to do?" Well, yes, except that, in order to give me this reminder, the brain does some other things I probably wouldn't want if I really knew what was happening.

Let's imagine that when my brain sets off the message, "Proof the report," it does not simply have the *words* "Proof the report" loop through

117

my mind. Let's suppose that it actually has me go through the *activity* of proofing the report in my head. My brain visualizes me actually doing the activity. I could use up quite a bit of mental energy in this rehearsal, almost as much as it would take to proof the report.

This scenario, in fact, comes close to what does happen in your head every time you see something you wish to do. You rehearse the activity in your mind. And energy is spent looking at it that could be spent doing it.

Moreover, there's another problem with visuals as mental reminders. While you're rehearsing one thing with your mind (because your eyes happen to see it), you're usually supposed to be doing something else with your body. For example, when Sarah glances into her rearview mirror to decide whether it's OK to pull back into the right-hand lane after passing a Mack truck, she also catches sight of the mound of clothes for the Salvation Army. So while her body is trying to handle speed and distance and dexterity, her mind, for a brief but nonetheless critical second, goes off to the Salvation Army. The tension of trying to "think" two things at once places another small chink in Sarah's already battered armor of nerves. A visual reminder has become a visual stressor.

Looking at things you want to do takes energy. When you are not in a position to actually *do* the task, this energy expenditure turns into stress and mental fatigue. No wonder you frequently find yourself exclaiming, "I get tired just looking at that stuff." You *are* tired just looking at that stuff. By running through the entire project in your head, the best activity you've probably prepared yourself for is a nap.

In short, visual stressors not only make us feel anxious in the moment. They also sap away energy so we don't get the projects done in the future. Sarah is so tired from looking at all those pictures that have to be pasted in the picture album that she has little energy left to actually paste the pictures in the album. She is so exhausted from constantly rehearsing all those "Remembers" over her desk that she is able to actually accomplish very little.

Which brings me to Organizing Adage 8:

> If you can't do it now,
> looking at it won't help you do it later.
> Looking at it will only make you tired.

ELIMINATING VISUAL STRESSORS

You eliminate visual stressors by putting them out of sight. Someplace. Anyplace. Just so long as they're not where you can see them and begin to "rehearse." You'll be surprised at what a positive difference it will make in how you feel and how much you get done.

The experience of one of my clients is a very clear example of this point. This client had been married for a year and a half, and the bulk of his wedding gifts were still piled in the spare room off the kitchen. He and his wife frequently glanced into this room through the open door as they went about preparing dinner in the evening. At least three times a week, one or the other would say, "We've got to sort through that stuff and put it away next Saturday." But Saturday after Saturday went by, and the stuff stayed put.

At the time I was consulting with his firm, my client was having an additional problem. He and his wife both worked, but they also both loved to cook. So they prepared meals together, using the time to catch up on the day, enjoy each other's company, and unwind.

In the last several months, however, dinnertime had started to turn sour. Meals were being burned. Spats were breaking out. And my client had actually started to worry about the stability of his marriage—until he heard me discuss the concept of visual stressors with his work group. Then a light went on in his head.

He realized that a roomful of unsorted wedding gifts was the ultimate guilt trip. He and his wife had been afraid to close the door, afraid they'd forget all about the gifts until Aunt Ida and Uncle Leo came to dinner and didn't see "their" vase. However, at my urging, when he went home that night, he closed the door to the spare room.

When I saw him at a follow-up session two weeks later, he was beaming. Things in the kitchen had improved 100 percent, and he and his wife were back on the track of good meals and good companionship. He commented that he didn't know when the room would get sorted out, but he really no longer worried about it. It had sat for over a year with nothing terrible happening. Eventually, it would get done.

A week later, when I was on-site consulting with another work group, this client came up to me looking very serious and pale. I was afraid that Aunt Ida and Uncle Leo had shown up to dinner and, not seeing their vase, had cut my client off from some huge inheritance. "I don't understand it," he began. "You remember my spare room, the one full of gifts, the one that's been sitting there for a year and a half? Well, last Saturday my wife said, 'Why don't we sort the gifts,' and I said 'OK,' and we cleaned up the whole project in three hours. I don't understand it. It's unbelievable. I don't know where the energy came from." And he shook my hand.

It's important for me to point out that rehearsal isn't always bad. Affirmations and visualizations are great methods for closing priority dissonance, for example. These methods are controlled, systematic uses of the brain's ability to rehearse.

But rehearsal from visual stressors is uncontrolled and unsystematic. It's set off when you can't do anything about the task and when you should be concentrating on something else (like carefully passing a Mack truck).

Some of you may worry about procrastination. "Out of sight, out of mind." If I put it away, it may never get done. Well, I would like to suggest that your procrastination increases because you *don't* put it away.

121

Procrastination arises from one of two sources: either I feel dislike for a task and therefore put it off, or I feel overloaded by a task and therefore put it off. Either way, looking at the task all the time simply increases my feelings of dislike and overload. In fact, visual stressors actually increase the overload by taking away energy that's needed for doing and using it up in rehearsing.

I recommend strongly that you get visual stressors out of sight so that they *will* be out of mind. Then your mind will be free to focus on the task at hand and have energy for the tasks to come.

When you put the stuff away, you unplug your brain from using rehearsal as a reminder mechanism. But then, how will you remind yourself to complete the task that is now in the drawer, the closet, or the trunk of the car? The reminder system recommended in most time-management books is a "to-do" list. Another alternative, the one I recommend, is to have and use a planner. I shall discuss these two systems, each in turn, in the next two chapters. I would like to close this chapter, however with:

THE MAIN POINT

Having piles of stuff lying around so you won't forget to do something doesn't get the "something" done. It just makes you tired. Put the stuff away someplace. Release yourself from rehearsing and let yourself get on with doing.

CHAPTER 8

The Problem with "To-Do" Lists

Traditional time-management techniques were first popularized with the publication of Alan Lakein's *How To Get Control of Your Time and Your Life* in 1973. Since then, literally hundreds of books, articles, workshops, and training films, as well as audio/video cassettes, have reworked, reworded, and re-presented various principles of time management. Virtually all of these presentations expound the virtues, in one form or another, of keeping a "to-do" list.

The to-do list is, in fact, a ubiquitous element that permeates every aspect of traditional time-management training. Setting priorities is supposedly facilitated by a to-do list. Conducting meetings effectively is supposedly facilitated by a to-do list. Breaking out of procrastination and even avoiding interruptions have, at times, been linked to keeping and using a to-do list. The rightness of the to-do list, like the goodness of motherhood, has become unquestioned and unquestionable conventional wisdom.

Now before the time-management movement popularized the to-do-list technique, most people were just trying to carry everything around in their heads or moving, unsystematically, from one activity to another with little or no planning or overview. Certainly, keeping to-do lists would appear to be an improvement over such conditions.

However, in the past fifteen or so years, a lot of people, influenced by the popularization of time management, have actually kept, or attempted to keep, to-do lists. The experiences of these people have given us a rich source of information on how to-do lists really work—not their theoretical effectiveness as presented in books or workshops, but their actual effectiveness as experienced by real people trying to cope with their real lives each day.

Observing these real-life experiences, I've come to the conclusion that to-do lists, while being better than nothing, do themselves generate three serious problems for the person who is trying to get and stay organized:

1. To-do lists are perpetual.

2. To-do lists don't prioritize, they "criticalize."

3. To-do lists are visual stressors.

OUR LADY OF PERPETUAL LISTS

I used to keep to-do lists. I kept them throughout undergraduate school and for nearly ten years thereafter. I prided myself on being "organized," and, in fact, was regarded as a paragon of organization by many around me.

However, I soon felt a growing concern. I was feeling less and less like a paragon and more and more like a drudge. Each morning I would make my list for the day. This list usually included items that had not been completed the previous day. In the morning, optimistic and energetic (I am one of those disgusting "morning" people), I would feel certain that I could take care of the old business and still have time to address a lot of new business, as well. So I added quite a few tasks to my list.

The next morning's list inevitably found me again with unfinished business and again with new things to be added. My concern grew into low-level anxiety. "If I'm so organized," I would worry, "why is it I never finish what has to be done?"

In fact, the list never ended. There was always something that, according to the list, had to be done "today." Whether the day was my birthday, Christmas, New Year's, or the Fourth of July, there was always a to-do list waiting, ongoing, perpetual. This list, lurking somewhere in my briefcase or desk drawer, threw a small cloud of guilt over these festive days. Time became an increasingly stressful race to see if I could possibly get through my lists. In fact, at one point, thinking back on my Roman Catholic background, I began to describe myself as a worshiper of "Our Lady of Perpetual Lists."

My "organizing self-esteem" fell lower and lower as my perpetual list went on and on. I never felt completely satisfied at the end of the day because I never felt completely finished at the end of the day.

To-do lists are a problem because they are perpetual. They deny our basic human need for a sense of closure and completion.

TO-DO LISTS DON'T PRIORITIZE, THEY "CRITICALIZE"

Talking with other persons who are or have been committed keepers of to-do lists, I've found a common pattern. This pattern has caused a serious problem for many to-do-list keepers. Maybe you have this problem yourself.

Trained in time management, you write out "things to do" each day. But in writing this list, you find that you write down not only what really *must* be done on that day but also what you *want* to do on that day.

OK. So far, so good. No problem with that. The problem enters in when you take what, for many of us, is the next step. Once something's on the list, you treat it as though it *has to* be completed that day, whether the thing is a "must" or not. In short, you "criticalize" everything. And designating every item as "critical" is not the most effective way to prioritize.

In fact, a daily to-do list can't possibly keep track of priorities. (Even those of us who were foolhardy enough to try to number the items on our lists in the order of their priorities or assign "A, B, C" designations to tasks soon found ourselves spending more time reordering and recopying our lists than actually doing the tasks!)

For one thing, it is impossible to gauge how long a particular project may take. Sometimes I can complete my weekly review of my firm's books in fifteen minutes. Other times it takes me more than an hour. It just depends.

Second, "life is what happens when you've made other plans." In the reality of day-to-day living, new tasks present themselves all the time. So an activity that was very important to you when you made your list may become less important as the day goes on and presents new opportunities and responsibilities. Sticking strictly to the list only dehumanizes you. You become rigid, inflexible, and basically less effective, especially when it comes to dealing with opportunities.

So most of us don't stick strictly to our list. And then we end up with a whole batch of "incompletes" at the end of the day. Our lists remain perpetual, and we feel like failures. It's a no-win situation.

CHAPTER 8

TO-DO LISTS AS VISUAL STRESSORS

After my comments in the last chapter, I think you
will be able to understand this point without too
much elaboration. What do you think happens
every time you look down that to-do list to decide
what to do next? What do you think happens every
time you recopy the list or "reorder" priorities on
the list? That's right, you got it: "mental rehearsal."

Every time you read a list of items indicating
things you have to do, you are "doing" each one
of those things in your head! No wonder so many
people find themselves looking through their to-do
lists, then deciding they need a cup of coffee before
they can "do" another thing. Reading the list has
exhausted them.

A to-do list is a visual stressor. It takes a lot of
energy to read that list, energy that could be spent
on doing the things that are on the list. In fact,
frequently consulting your to-do list may be
another reason why your to-do list never gets done.

WITHOUT A TO-DO LIST,
WHAT AM I TO DO?

To be organized, it is essential to have a system
for recalling what we must do and what we wish
to do. Most of us cannot successfully hold all that
information in our heads. However, effective organizing requires that this system be constructive
and systematic, designed to limit the amount of

rehearsal, automatically prioritize each task, and accommodate unexpected opportunities and responsibilities.

I still keep lists, but I keep them in a very special way. I keep a planner. We will consider, in the next chapter, how a properly-constructed planner system can be used to support effective organizing in your life.

THE MAIN POINT

To-do lists can cause as many problems as they were invented to solve. My to-do list can become a perpetual visual stressor that turns everything I have to do into top-priority status. A planner system is a way for me to overcome these problems. A properly constructed planner system keeps me from criticalizing, rehearsing, and dehumanizing my life. I've got more energy available to get things done. And then, at the end of the day, I can feel satisfied with what I have accomplished.

CHAPTER 9

Planners: What They Are and How to Use Them

A quiet and very interesting phenomenon is moving throughout American business. This phenomenon manifests itself in the increasing numbers of people, involved in all kinds of occupations, who always carry and use *"the book"*:

- Last week, when the tiler, Leo Scott, arrived to repair my bathroom tiles, I noticed that he was carrying a small blue version of the book along with his tool chest and caulking materials. When I mentioned that I had the book, as well (a medium-sized purple version), Leo exclaimed that the book was "the best thing my wife ever bought me. Everything is organized, laid out just nice," he continued. And he was right. In his book, Leo not only had all his appointments, suppliers' phone numbers, and copies of estimates. He even had graph paper on which to plot out room designs when he made the estimates.

- Several months ago, I was exchanging some tickets at the Albany Airport counter of Bar Harbor Airways. As I removed the tickets from my book, Elvita Brown, Bar Harbor Airways ticket agent, exclaimed, "You've got the book!" She then told me that she had ordered the book last week, received it yesterday, and was already thrilled at feeling an increased sense of organization in her life. When I told her I was doing some writing on organizing, she enthusiastically offered to show me her book, a small maroon version. Elvita had already made entries in the priorities section. "I'm going to spend this evening setting it up," she said. "I can't wait. Having this book feels great!"

- Last year, I received a call from the training and development director of a corporation where I had completed an extensive assessment and development program six months before. The program had involved organizing-skills training, including instructions on the whats, whys, and hows of using the book. The majority of the administrative support, technical, and middle-management staff had completed the course. Upper management, on the other hand, had explained that it didn't have the time to take the training.

The training and development director informed me that now, however, upper management did want the training, and would I come back and conduct another cycle of assessment and workshops. Apparently, a particular vice-president, an influential figure in the upper echelon, had noticed an increasing number of staff people carrying and using the book. These books were of varying sizes and colors. Some were commercial. Some appeared to be homemade. But the unifying factor seemed to be that each of these books was enabling its owner to get things done with more effectiveness and less flurry.

At staff meetings, the vice-president saw people speaking from notes in their books. During project planning conferences, he saw people writing comments into their books. When she gave him his morning briefing, his secretary read from a page in her book. As the vice-president walked up and down the halls, at meetings, conferences, casual chats, he saw more and more staff carrying and using the book. Finally, he stuck his head into the training and development director's office and asked, "When can we get together so you can tell me what is this book everybody is carrying?" The training and development director then took out his book.

WHAT IS "THE BOOK"?

The generic name for the book is a *planner*. A planner is a physical system of organization. It provides a coherent and reliable means of recording the arrangements you have made concerning priorities, people, information, space, and physical objects.

Many people try to carry around the details of their arrangements in their heads. Given the extraordinary amount of details present in the average American life, and the rapidity with which these details often change, it is no wonder that these people frequently feel crazy.

Other people do write down their arrangements. But they tend to write them all over the place: slips of paper in pockets and pocketbooks, desk calendars, bulletin boards, to-do lists. Then, when they need to recall the details of their arrangements, they have to plow through several different "systems" to track them down. And frequently, they're never found, or at least not found when needed. Needless to say, these people, too, often feel crazy.

The answer to these two problems is to store all the details of all your arrangements in one book: a planner. A planner allows you to collapse the multiple, inefficient methods of remembering you've created for yourself into one, efficient, effective system.

When you have and use a planner, the book, not your brain, carries the burden of remembering. You have a system that works with you rather than against you. As Organizing Adage 9 puts it:

Move it out of your head
and into your book.

WHAT EVERY GOOD PLANNER SHOULD HAVE

Dozens of commercial planners are on the market today. They vary in style, color, materials, and significantly, in price. You can purchase a planner for $20.00 all the way up to $350.00 Even with all these variations, there are, nevertheless, some basic elements any planner should have if it is to function as an effective organizing system. Whether you make your planner or buy your planner, whether you pay $300.00 or $30.00, make sure the planner has all of the following features.

Ring-Binder Cover with Open-Close Rings

Your planner should adjust and adapt to your organizing needs. You require the flexibility of creating new sections, deleting irrelevant sections, and moving sections around. You can't do this when the book has a fixed binding. Along the same lines, it's nice if the planner has standard dimensions— for example, 5" × 7" or 8½" × 11"—with standard hole-punch spacing. Then, you can design sections with commercial stationery without the expense of buying specially sized paper from the planner company. If you intend to carry any standard-size documents in your system (attendance sheets, monthly reports, vacation schedules), the planner dimensions should definitely be standard.

Separate Sections for Priority Categories

Mary Kubic, president of Organize and Live, has commented, "The beginning of organization . . . is to find out what is important in your life and what is unimportant at any given time and to be able to differentiate the two." Your planner must have clearly defined, separate sections that distinguish the level of importance of any task at any given time.

As I mentioned in the previous chapter, giant, undifferentiated to-do lists do not fit this bill. Most commercial planners have a section on each page of the daily calendar where you can write a to-do list.

You do not want "to do" this list. Instead, add three sections to the planner, each section marked by a tab, that indicate three levels of priorities. You can use a "1," "2," "3" system; a "high," "medium," "low" system; a "red," "green," "blue" system—any designation you wish. Then, whenever you are requested to do something or think of something yourself, write it down in one of the sections.

After you are sure there are priority sections in your planner, your next step is to assign criteria to each priority. Write a descriptive statement for each one: "A task is priority 1 if . . ." "A task is low-priority if . . ."

Organize and Live Consulting recommends the following three priority categories and their definitions:

- *Critical*: tasks that must be done within twenty-four hours or you will lose your job or the affection of someone you care about.

- *Soon*: tasks that should be completed in seven days or you will lose your job or the affection of someone you care about.

- *Anytime*: everything else—tasks that you must do or wish to do at some future date.

"Critical" projects should be attacked in the first part of the day. You will feel calm and function better for the rest of the day, knowing that what absolutely must be done has been done. Interruptions and crises will be less anxiety-provoking.

"Soon" and "anytime" projects are important, but they don't need to be completed today. Some people worry that they will have pages and pages of "anytimes" or "priority 3s" or "blues." But remember, "anytime" tasks should not be a source of pressure. Trust your telic nature. Remember, if it's of value to you, you will, eventually, do it. And if the task has no value to you, well, then, maybe you shouldn't force yourself to do it at all.

In fact, the anytime section is a wonderful holding and evaluating tool. Reviewing this section, I get to redetermine whether I really want to do each task or not. There have been at least three instances since I've been using a planner where "anytime" tasks became "no time" tasks: I realized these activities had no real value or meaning for me, so I crossed them out.

You should review each priority section once a day to get an overview of what's happened and to monitor "soons'" becoming "criticals" and "any-times'" becoming "soons."

However, because the planners separate the crucial from the less crucial, you don't have to be reminded of those less crucial items until you're ready to deal with them. In fact, once you complete and cross off all your "criticals," you are faced with a blank page! There is nothing left that you "must" do today. At this point, you can either turn to the "soons" or do nothing!

On at least two occasions, I have looked at my empty "critical" page and decided to take a mental-health day and "do nothing." The day was enjoyed without guilt because I knew I hadn't forgotten anything and because I knew that the next day the planner system would let me pick right up where I left off. Most of the time, however, an empty "critical" page stirs up in me a feeling of relief and energy to go on to the "soons" and frequently to the "anytimes."

Finally, it's OK to write down dates next to priorities, but don't number them. Given the realities of life, you may never be done writing in and changing numbers. Instead, simply review the priority section; pick the thing you have the time, energy, and motivation to do; and do it. It's amazing how the deities will let you know who should be next. And it's amazing how much you can accomplish using this priority approach.

Daily Calendar

Use it for fixed appointments, but don't write in

unscheduled "to-do" activities. If you do, you will probably list many more than you can finish in a given day. This "failure" causes you to feel pressured. So be nice to yourself by not making a daily to-do list. Use the daily calendar only for scheduled appointments and let the priority sections take care of the rest.

By the way, if you have regularly occurring weekly activities (meetings, music lessons, barber, or beautician), you don't have to spend time recopying (and sometimes miscopying) these appointments each week. Using a Post-it slip, write "Go to staff meeting, 10:30" on it, and under that write, "Reschedule . . ." If your meetings are every Tuesday, post this reminder on next Tuesday's calendar. Then just move it every week thereafter.

Month at a Glance

Important for planning blocks of time and getting an overview of arrangements.

Event Calendar

The event calendar is twelve pages or twelve sections on a page, one for each month of the year. It is the place to record yearly recurring events: sales campaigns, annual meetings, your pet's booster shots at the vet, the inspection due date for the car. The event calendar is the only section of your planner that is more or less permanent. You can "post" a reminder to yourself on a certain day of the month in the daily calendar to review the event calendar for the next month.

Goals

I have discussed at length in this book the importance of knowing and understanding your goals. In the planner system, your operational goals are recorded in the priorities and daily calendar sections of the planner. Your theoretical priorities are recorded in what is usually called the goals section of the planner.

By having these two important pieces of information together in one system, you can more easily monitor and correct priority dissonance. It is important that you reread your goals once a day. Then, if your priorities and appointments are not moving you toward your goals, it's time to rethink the situation. You may decide that some goals simply have to be put on the back burner for a while. But by rereading your goals each day, these deities are at least acknowledged. And as you recall, keeping deities acknowledged is very, very important.

Persons

The persons section provides a system for recording information you wish to transmit to someone else. A separate sheet of paper is assigned to each person in your life with whom you frequently exchange information. Then, whenever you think of something you wish to tell that person or ask that person, instead of interrupting yourself and the person because you "don't want to forget," you write down the information on that person's sheet.

Then, decide how often you need to exchange information with this person. Get together twice a day, once a day, once a week, or whatever is appropriate. If the other individual keeps a "person" sheet for you, as well, all the better. When the time comes to meet, take your planner, or just that person's sheet, and exchange notes. You'll be able to make all your comments and ask all your questions without forgetting any and without causing interruptions.

Incidentally, persons pages are extremely effective for exchanging information with people outside of work. The persons pages I keep for my doctor, my accountant, and my auto mechanic have saved me a significant amount of time, worry, and money.

Project

In this section, you can include a page or pages to track the ideas you have, resources you need, and steps you have completed for various projects. For example, in my planner, I have several project pages for this book. On these pages I have jotted down ideas as they occur to me and resources that have been referred to me. I also have a project page headed "Ideas for Articles," a page labeled "Yard Restoration," and another simply called "Vacation."

Telephone Numbers and Addresses

Included here are the numbers you use the most. This section is essential when you're away from home and office and need to contact someone. It basically replaces your old address book.

The telephone and address section, the calendars, person and project sections, as well as the information in a personal profile section which includes data such as your insurance and credit card number, work together in such a way that your planner becomes a portable office.

THE MAIN POINT

A planner offers an effective means for keeping track of all your arrangements of priorities, people, information, space, and physical objects. A planner facilitates functional organizing because a planner takes all of these arrangements out of your head and off slips of paper, bulletin boards, and refrigerator doors and orders them into one comprehensive and comprehensible system.

In Appendix B, I've included a list of several companies that sell planners and a brief description of the products they offer. You may wish to purchase a planner from one of these firms. On the other hand, you may wish to make your own planner (some of the most effective planners I have seen have been "handmade"). Whether you buy a planner or make one, get a planner. The ability of the book to improve your organizing systems is truly amazing.

CHAPTER 10

Organizing
the Organization:
Some Closing Reflections

Looking back over the last nine chapters, I realize that we have taken quite a journey through and around the topic of organizing. Our exploration has introduced us to telic natures, collective structures, retroactive meanings, priority dissonance, gods, goddesses, planners, and many other strange and exciting entities. I've led you on this journey in the hope that, through awareness and utilization of these ideas, you may enhance the order, meaningfulness, and joy of your work. Work is too important for it to be meaningless and sad.

Throughout the book, my comments have had a dual focus:

1. On the individual in the organization.

2. On the work group in the organization.

These two different areas of focus can be regarded as two different levels of organizing systems. Effectively solving organizing problems involves correctly identifying at what level each problem resides.

Although work groups are comprised of individuals, organizations are comprised of work groups. In other words, work groups do the organizing in most organizations. Therefore, the work group is the most valid level of focus for most organizing problems in most organizations.

Moreover, a collection of well-organized individuals does not necessarily add up to a well-organized work group. Why? Because work-group goals do not necessarily correspond to individual goals. Moreover, the arrangement of resources required by the organization to meet its goals may not correspond to the arrangement of resources required by the individual to meet his or her goals.

This lack of correspondence increases the likelihood that the goals of the work group will not make sense to the telic, meaning-oriented members of that group. Consequently, these members will be unable to collectively create the work-group arrangements necessary to meet the work-group goals.

Organizations cannot meet the challenge of generating and sustaining functional organizing systems by labeling isolated individuals as "disorganized" and shipping them off to time-management training. Even if every single member of the organization were to successfully complete the best time-management training in the world, the return on this enormous investment would drop when these staff members moved from the individual to the group level of organizing.

In fact, many of you have probably observed the phenomenon of colleagues who express indifference and boredom at the idea of "more time-management courses" on the one hand while on the other anxiously request some guidance on "how we can get organized around here." The problem is that your colleagues have received more than enough training at the individual level, while they have received virtually no training at the group level. *And it is at the group level that they are charged with organizing the organization.*

As Sue Gould, president of the Los Angeles-based Professional Resources Group recently pointed out to a meeting of senior corporate executives, "Throughout our society, employees and managers alike are bombarded with 'you are defied to survive' challenges created by inflation, . . . conflict of personal versus company goals, potential burnout and myriad other 'slice of life' stress factors. We can only meet these challenges by empowering ourselves to seek out the resources we need to fulfill our vast untapped potential." In other words, the challenge of generating and sustaining functional organizing systems for the organization can be met only when work groups are trained *as a group.* The work group must be trained to design and redesign forms of social organization that will identify individual purposes and arrangements. It can then link these purposes and arrangements to each other and to the purposes of the organization. Moreover, this matrix of purposes and arrangements should be designed in such a way that the entire system is sensible, although not necessarily agreeable, to each member of the group.

Organizing Skills Training, for example, a program designed by my consulting firm, is a resource available to work groups that have empowered themselves to meet the challenge of being a functional organizing system. Organizing Skills Training teaches work groups how to make sense of their current arrangements and create new arrangements that make better sense. Whatever training resources you offer, however, the main point is that the program be offered to the work group as a group, because the work group is the valid level of organizing training in organizations.

Some of you may worry: "But what about the disorganized individuals? After all, they *do* exist. Are you suggesting that I offer no individually focused programs?"

I am not suggesting the abolition of individual time-management training programs. However, individuals are subsumed within work groups, and therefore, training at the group level includes individual training, whereas the opposite is not true: individual training does not logically lead to work-group training.

In other words, what I am suggesting is that you initiate your assessment and correction of organizing skills at the work-group level. Then, after this intervention, you can determine whether additional individual training is still needed by some persons.

The main point here is to watch out for the "quick fix." Even when the self-labeled "disorganized person" asks for a time-management course, we need to remember that this person is part of a system, his or her work group. Before we assume that the problem is with, and therefore can be fixed at the level of, the individual, it behooves us to check out the level of the work group.

SOMETIMES IT'S NEITHER THE INDIVIDUAL NOR THE WORK GROUP . . .

Stephen Schuit, human resource manager at Digital Equipment Corporation, has observed: "Poll a group of training professionals or other managers concerning how they handle requests for help with what appear to be time-management problems. Probably 90 to 95 percent will say that they send employees to a time-management workshop. But the fact is that frequently what individuals or departments see as their own individual time-management problems, these problems are really symptoms of much larger organizational issues— issues such as lack of corporate direction, unclear (or unknown!) strategic goals, or poor control systems." Schuit's comments are another way of saying that some work groups experience dysfunctional organizing because they are attempting to operate in a dysfunctioning organization.

The organization represents the third level of assessment and correction. The organization consists of a system of work groups. When organizing dysfunction is assessed at the level of the organization, the appropriate correction is a program of developing the organization, rather than simply training the work groups and individuals. Why? Because the logic suggested earlier in this chapter applies here, as well: a collection of organized work groups does not necessarily result in an organized company.

Organizational development consists of a program of purposeful and systematic steps to improve the functioning of the company as a whole. Organizational development is not a few workshops on time management. A few workshops on time management will not correct a dysfunctioning organization.

An excellent example of organizational development issues disguised as time-management issues occurred in my own consulting practice. Four years ago, I received a call from a divisional operations director of a major international corporation. This director had heard something about my work and had finally decided to call me. Things had gotten out of hand in his division, and although he was skeptical, he didn't know what else to do at this point: he wanted me to come out and "give a couple of time-management workshops" to his entire staff.

When I asked him to expand a bit upon the things that were out of hand, he explained that everybody was working unacceptably long hours. Last month, the professional staff had hit an average of one hundred hours a week. "Obviously, they don't know how to plan their time," he said.

Everybody was covering two or three areas of responsibility because nobody was efficiently assigning work to subordinates. "Obviously, they don't know how to delegate," he said.

Everybody was leaving meetings with no clear sense of what had happened at the meetings or, worse, with the wrong sense of what had happened. "Obviously, they don't know how to run meetings," he said.

From what the director told me, I did not feel it would be valid or professionally ethical for me to simply go in there, offer a two-day workshop, and leave him with the impression that all his problems were now "obviously" solved. I explained to him my wish to perform an organizational assessment before conducting any training. Then, I could design a program that would be right for his firm.

After some discussion, he agreed to allow me to perform an assessment. The assessment involved interviewing a sample of the staff, submitting a paper-and-pencil questionnaire to everyone, and employing several observational measures. The results were powerful, sensible, and indicated some different "obvious" areas in need of correction.

The major area of organizational dysfunction in this division turned out to be lack of succession planning and management. The reason people didn't delegate was because there was no one to delegate to. There had been a failure to ensure that an adequate number of foremen moved up to first-line-supervisor level. Thus, there was a critical lack of what one interviewee called "noncommissioned officers"—people at lower levels of management who could handle routine tasks.

Thus, the upper-management staff covered two or three bases and worked a hundred hours a week. Meanwhile, the foremen were grumbling because they weren't "moving up." Moreover, since this situation had been building for several years, two key upper managers had simply burned out and quit the organization. A third person was on the verge. These occurrences had seriously undermined the motivation and morale of the group, as well as its ability to communicate and work together as a team. People were too tired, too upset, and too scared to really focus on what was happening in a meeting.

Upon reviewing my report, senior management recognized that the true level of dysfunction was the organization itself. Together we designed and conducted an organizational development program to correct the dislocation. Over a period of two years, through a series of structure and process interventions—including the establishment of a formal performance and career-planning program, the promotion of three foremen to first-line supervisors, and two off-site weekend retreats—the division not only survived but learned how to thrive as a self-assessing, self-correcting system. And to my knowledge, the division has yet to offer a time-management workshop.

CORPORATE CULTURE CONFUSION: PRIORITY DISSONANCE ON A GRAND SCALE

Corporate culture is the pattern of how things are done in an organization. As Lawrence Bennyson states in his article "Managing Corporate Cultures," "If finance, operations and marketing are examples of a corporation's 'hard' system, culture is the sum of its 'soft' systems, the beliefs and values that guide an organization in its day-to-day activities."

For an organization, as for an individual, beliefs and values are expressed as theoretical priorities and operational priorities. Theoretical priorities are expressed through statements of goals—for example, in strategic plans, business plans, and long-range budgets. Operational priorities are expressed through the things the organization actually does—reflected in quarterly reports, minutes of meetings, and operating budgets.

Dissonance and subsequent organizational dysfunction occur when an organization expresses one set of theoreticals while making arrangements of resources (time, people, money, space) that support a different set of operationals. Priority dissonance at the organization level often occurs when a company is evolving from one stage to another

151

in what Larry Greiner, associate professor of organizational behavior at Harvard Business School, calls "phases of growth and crisis."

Greiner suggests that the first phase of organizational growth is marked by individual creativity. A company will continue to grow through creativity until it has the crisis related to creativity, a crisis of leadership. In other words, all of those creative individuals need coordinating if the organization is to move in a consistent and coherent direction.

If the company survives the crisis of leadership—that is, if a structure of authority is allowed to emerge—the company will move into the second stage of organizational growth, growth through direction. Growth will continue until directing and controlling systems become so prevalent and complex that virtually all authority and responsibility rest at the top. The organization becomes overdirected, increasingly inflexible, and slow to respond to stimuli, from both within and from without. This situation results in the phase-two crisis of autonomy. If the organization survives this crisis, it moves into its third developmental phase, growth through delegation.

Although Greiner postulates five phases, a look at the first two can suggest to us the relationship between organizational growth, priority dissonance, and dysfunctional organizing arrangements in a company. Specifically, a first-phase organization will experience dissonance during that period when its strategic plans, reports to stockholders, and other "theoretical" statements continue to support individual creativity, while its performance reviews, budget allocations, and other "operationals" move toward more centralized direction and control. Why?

Because people within an organization look toward the top for signals about what is important. When I, top management, am giving contradictory signals because I am in a crisis of organizational growth, some work groups will "do as I do," and some work groups will "do as I say to do." Work groups will be operating at cross-purposes concerning the desired values and outcomes for the organization. Just as important, there will be conflict over what arrangements of people, information, time, space, and physical objects are acceptable vehicles for achieving these outcomes. The result will be a dysfunctional, "disorganized" organization, and all the time-management courses in the world won't help. What will help is an organizational development program to move the company successfully through its crisis phase into its next phase of growth and thus bring the organization's theoreticals and operationals back into harmony again.

IN CLOSING . . .

I would like to reissue the warning I gave in the Introduction to this book: Don't meddle yourself or your organization into a mess.

CHAPTER 10

Many of the ideas I've suggested here may sound new, intriguing, and inviting to you. But I urge you, no matter what the company across town is doing, no matter what the work group down the hall is doing, no matter what the person who gave you this book is doing, trust your own telic nature. Adopt the ideas offered here only if they fit *your* situation and make sense to *you*. I have attempted to offer here not so much a "how-to" book as a "why-to" book. If some of the concepts do have meaning for you, if you sense that they somehow can enhance the "why" of your organizing systems, then go ahead and try them.

Because, as the last organizing adage, Organizing Adage 10, observes (with due acknowledgment to Nietzsche):

A person who has a "why" to live
can bear with almost any "how."

APPENDIX A

Ten Adages to Organize By

TEN ADAGES TO ORGANIZE BY

We all use our time
to get something.

•

People and objects, space and time
are interconnected.
If you want to change the arrangement of one and can't,
change the arrangement of another.
It will help.

•

If you want to know how to organize your life,
look at what's important to you.

•

If it doesn't make sense to you,
you won't do it.
And if you're doing it,
then, at some level,
it *is* making sense to you.

•

If you want to know what's important to you,
look at how you use your time.

157

Your brain hears
what your mouth says.

•

To get it all together,
acknowledge that it's all apart.

•

If you can't do it now,
looking at it won't help you do it later.
Looking at it will only make you tired.

•

Move it out of your head
and into your book.

•

A person who has a "why" to live
can bear with almost any "how."

APPENDIX B

Where to Get Planners

Recently, I received a mail-order catalog containing an advertisement for a planner system. The ad declared that planners were "the latest time-management fad," that planner companies were "coming out of the woodwork," but that the planner sold through this catalog was "unquestionably the best system in the world."

Now it's true that more and more people are using planners these days, and that there are dozens of planner companies. However, there is no such thing as the "best system in the world."

Different planners have different features, and different people need different features to meet their unique organizing requirements. The best planner for Juanita, project engineer, may not be the best planner for Karl, flower-shop owner.

Take, for example, the question of size. (Planners come in 3½" × 6¾", 5½" × 8½", and 8½" × 11".) Or the question of color. (Planner covers run the gamut from tanned glove leather to magenta vinyl.)

In this section, I describe nine planner systems. I have personally examined each planner listed, and all of the systems meet the basic requirements for a planner outlined in chapter 9 except for the matter of to-do lists. Only the Organize and Live planner has predesignated critical, soon, and anytime sections. All the other systems use a to-do-list format. So you will have to insert your own priority sections.

Finally, I know that some of you would really like to know what planner system *I* use. Well, for me to name names might influence your decision, and I wouldn't want to do that. What's best for me might not be best for you.

I will tell you, though, that four years ago I started with a system that worked very well for me. Over time, however, my requirements changed, and I switched to another system, keeping several components of the first. At present, this hybrid is right for me. I sincerely hope that you will be able to identify or create a planner system that is right for you.

DAY RUNNER

Harper House, Inc.
3562 Eastham Drive
Culver City, California 90232
1 (800) 2DAY RUN
1 (800) 8DAY RUN (California)

Price: $45.00.

Size: 5½″ × 8½″.

Color: Choice of eighteen colors, from turquoise vinyl to wine hide and black dragonskin at additional cost.

Comments: Includes a supply of dated monthly calendar pages for the year and a three-month supply of undated daily calendar pages. Velcro flap closure. Ruler/page marker. Inside cover includes pockets for checkbook, calculator, spare keys, and business cards, as well as a pen and notepad.

DAY-TIMER 5-IN-1 JR. DESK SYSTEM

Day-Timers, Inc.
P.O. Box 2368
Allentown, Pennsylvania 18001
(215) 395-5884

Price: $16.95 for fillers and storage binder; $15.00 for desk binder.

Size: 5½″× 8½″.

Colors: Black, brown, and burgundy vinyl, as well as tanned glove cowhide and pigskin at additional cost.

Comments: Includes one-year supply of dated daily calendar pages and dated monthly calendar pages. Forty-seven-page handbook on how to use the system. Two-pages-per-day format (one-page-per-day and two-pages-per-week formats also available).

DELTA TIME MANAGEMENT AND PROJECT PLANNING SYSTEM

Los Altos Training and Development
565 University Avenue
Los Altos, California 94022
(415) 948-0196

Price: $130.00.

Size: 8½″×11″.

Color: Royal blue.

Comments: Includes one-year supply of dated monthly calendar pages, as well as supply of undated weekly and daily calendar pages in a plastic filing/storage case. Two-pages-per-year annual planning charts, enough for three years. Project-planner forms, including marketing, delegation, meetings, and communication pages for each project.

ORGANIZE AND LIVE DAILY PLANNER

Organize and Live Consulting
108 Jackson Avenue
Cohoes, New York 12047
(518) 235-7247

Price: $35.00.

Size: 5½" × 8½".

Color: Brown vinyl.

Comments: Includes one-year supply of dated daily and monthly calendar pages. Twenty-seven-page instruction section. Two-pages-per-day format.

RUNNING MATE

Harper House, Inc.
3562 Eastham Drive
Culver City, California 90232
1 (800) 2DAY RUN
1 (800) 8DAY RUN (California)

Price: $49.00.

Size: 3¾" × 6¾".

Color: Same as Day Runner.

Comments: Includes a supply of dated monthly calendar pages for the year and a three-month supply of undated daily calendar pages. Velcro flap closure. Ruler/page marker. Inside cover includes pockets for checkbook, calculator, spare keys, and business cards, as well as a pen and notepad.

TIME/DESIGN MANAGEMENT SYSTEM

Time/Design, Inc.
2101 Wilshire Boulevard
Santa Monica, California 90403
1 (800) 637-9942

Price: $135.00.

Color: Black textured vinyl.

Size: 5¾" × 8½".

Comments: Includes one-year supply of dated daily, weekly, and monthly calendar pages. Extra forms come in a plastic file/form storage container. Twenty-one pages of instructions. Daily and monthly project-overview sheets unfold to 8½" × 11". Project management and business meeting notes sections. Ruler/page marker. A mechanical pencil, as well as pockets for calculator, business cards, and miscellaneous papers on the inside cover.

TIME MAKER

Time Maker, Inc.
1150 First Avenue
King of Prussia, Pennsylvania 19406
(215) 265-5958

Price: $24.95.

Size: 6¾" × 4½".

Color: Embossed burgundy vinyl (available in leather with a brass clasp for $59.95).

Comments: One-year supply of dated monthly calendar pages. Three-month supply of undated daily calendar pages. Velcro flap closure. Household, groceries, menu planner, and diet forms and sections. Pen, as well as pockets for calculator, checks, and business cards, on inside covers.

TIME/SYSTEMS

Time/Systems, Inc.
5151 North 16th Street
No. D114
Phoenix, Arizona 85016
1 (800) 223-TIME

Price: $195.00.

Size: 8½" × 11" or 5½" × 8½".

Color: Deep brown leather-texture vinyl.

Comments: One-year supply of dated monthly calendar pages, six-month supply of undated daily calendar pages in record-storage file case. A "1–31" daily file section. A plan form and an activities form for each day. Price includes a half-day training workshop on the system if nine or more people order together.

TIME/SYSTEMS PROJECT MANAGEMENT

Time/Systems, Inc.
5151 North 16th Street
No. D114
Phoenix, Arizona 85016
1 (800) 223-TIME

Price: $125.00.

Size: 8½" × 11".

Color: Deep brown leather-texture vinyl.

Comments: Includes a three-month supply of planning worksheets, performance evaluations, project assignment sheets, and timetables in a lockable retention clasp binder. Price includes a half-day training workshop in the system if nine or more people order together.